What people are

How To Get Off Your Backside And Live your Life!

I love this book! Joyce has managed to distil her vast knowledge and experience into a potent mix of exercises and techniques that really can make a difference, and has laid them out in an easy to follow and logical way. This book is the next best thing to having your very own life coach on tap 24/7. If you follow the 7 steps in this book, it will work! This book is an investment that can only grow and grow.

Catherine O'Hare: O'Hare Associates

Joyce is one of the most authentic people I know. She walks her talk on a daily basis, and is an inspirational coach and trainer. If you get the opportunity to work with her, then grab it with both hands! Until then, this book is the next best thing to having her actually by your side. It's an inspiring mix of anecdotes, case studies, and exercises that work. Use this book, and be amazed to see how much you can transform your life.

Fraser Kerr

I have always admired Joyce for her drive and success. I am so pleased that she is now sharing the techniques she uses with her clients to enable those who can't get coaching in person to benefit from her skills. I'm looking forward to wearing this book out as I use it to improve my life with Joyce's help.

Jax Blunt

As a coach and trainer, Joyce has a no nonsense/no excuses approach. At the same time her compassion, enthusiasm and care for you shines through in everything she says and does. She really does want you to be all you can be, and she is totally on your side. This book takes the same approach, and it's the next best thing to having her as your personal coach.

Alex Hamilton

This fantastic book is so jam-packed with effective tools for changing your life, that if it were an actual toolkit, it would be way too heavy to carry! Already it has me thinking differently about how to change things that are holding me back, and got me making plans. It is a book that requires commitment, (which Joyce shows you how to maximise) and motivation (and there are some powerful exercises for increasing this). This book helps you every step along the way, and will richly reward you for everything you put into it.

Joanna Ratcliffe Goldie

In the years I have known Joyce, she has been a living testimony to all that NLP and coaching can offer. While facing challenges and hurdles she has walked her talk and remained strong, focused and positive. She is all the things she encourages you to be for yourself: a cheerleader, a constructive critic, a challenger and a great support. If you could learn to be all of that for yourself, then your life would be a happy one. Joyce is an inspirational woman, and this shines through in the book – she truly wants you to be all that you can.

Nic Goddard

How
To
Live
Your

get off your
backside
and

7 simple
steps
to transform
your life
using NLP,
Coaching
and
Hypnosis

Life!

Joyce H Campbell

lıp

First published in 2010 by:

Live It Publishing
27 Old Gloucester Road
London, United Kingdom.
WC1N 3AX
www.liveitpublishing.com

ISBN 978-1-906954-11-6 (pbk)

To Bob and Hannah, the lights of my life.

And in memory of my sister, Gillian Mary Campbell.
Never forgotten.

ACKNOWLEDGEMENTS

I have met many inspirational teachers since I started this exciting journey more than 20 years ago. Two however deserve special mention. Wilf Proudfoot, who lit the fire, and who will always have a special place 'in my hopper' and in my heart; and Dr Susi Strang who went that extra mile at a time when I needed it most, and in helping to close one circle, also opened the potential of the next one. Thank you.

My parents, Frank and Mary Campbell, who gave me roots, and then gave me wings.

My own personal dream team of friends, students and colleagues who provided regular cheerleading and who commented on the book in various stages of its development. They are: Katy Beresford, Jax Blunt, Nic Goddard, Helen Johnson, Maureen Mulligan, Catherine O'Hare of O'Hare Associates, and Colin Shaw of New Day Hypnosis.

Joanna Ratcliffe Goldie who not only commented on an early draft, but then proofread the final manuscript and sorted out my somewhat creative spelling and punctuation to make the finished product much more elegant.

My many students and clients, who over the years have taught me what it is all really about. Without them there could be no book.

And finally, my husband, Robert Westwater, and my daughter, Hannah. Thank you Bob for always being on my side. And Hannah, who taught me to be a mother, and a better human being. I hope you feel you chose well. Love you both.

CONTENTS

A WORD FROM JOYCE CAMPBELL

Over 30 years ago I set off to university to study psychology. I had some vague notion that this slightly trendy subject would help me understand people better. By the time I graduated, I knew more about laboratory rats than I did about people. I decided to channel my passion for working with people into nursing, and while doing that, took counselling training. But I still felt there had to be more.

One day I was browsing in a charity shop, and a book called *Frogs into Princes* by Richard Bandler and John Grinder quite literally fell off a shelf onto my head. I had found my answer. Within weeks I had started the first of many NLP trainings and kick-started a career in NLP, hypnotherapy and coaching.

Since then, I've become a Hypnotherapist, a Master Practitioner of NLP, a Master Coach, an MBTI practitioner and a trainer of NLP, Hypnotherapy and Coaching. I now train people to be Hypnotherapists, NLP practitioners and Coaches, and I continue to see private and corporate clients. I am still passionate about what I do, and *How To Get Off Your Backside And Live Your Life!* is a means of bringing some of the powerful tools I use with my clients to a wider audience.

The book is about the practical application of NLP, coaching and hypnosis, as used in my own work over more than two decades. I do not claim any intellectual ownership of the underpinning concepts, many of which are grounded in the work of Richard Bandler and John Grinder, the original developers of NLP; and in the work of Tad James in relation to Time Line Therapy™. I have also been inspired by the work of some great coaches.

I'm grateful to those trainers who have contributed to my learning and development over the years, and provided the inspiration for this work. They are, in the order I met them: Wilf Proudfoot, Steve and Connirae Andreas, Robert Dilts, Richard Bandler, Carol Sommer, Stephen Brooks, Ernest Rossi, Tony Robbins, Tad James, Stephen Buckbee, Tom McKay, Wyatt Woodsmall, Dr Susi Strang, Craig Wood, and David Shephard.

While I have made every attempt to provide appropriate acknowledgments and references for original sources where I know them, it is hard now to disentangle the sources in many years of study and learning. If you are aware of original sources, then please do contact us and we will ensure they are included in future editions of this book.

For more information about training courses, workshops, speaking engagements or personal consultations, visit us at www.joycecampbell.co.uk.

I wish you well.

Joyce Campbell

Scotland
20 June 2010

WELCOME!

A friend recently said to me 'someone else is living my life – I hope they are only breaking it in for me, because I would really like it back now'. Can you identify with that sentiment? Do you ever feel that surely there must be more to life than this? Do you ever ask yourself how you got here? Does the future sometimes look dull and uninspiring?

This is a book that has YOU at its heart. In seven simple steps, you will find techniques for letting go of the past, realistically assessing your present, and for creating a wonderful future. You will learn how to be the coach that you deserve – not just for a few sessions, but for life. I believe that good coaching is priceless. Nevertheless, the actual cost of coaching can be out of the reach of some budgets. The aim of this book is to put the tools and techniques a coach would use into your hands, so that you can learn to coach yourself. As you work through this book, you will have new experiences, new growth, new thoughts, and new learning. This book has the potential to assist you to make all the changes you want in order to help you live the life you were born to live.

> *Deep down in every human heart is a hidden longing, impulse and ambition to do something fine and enduring.*
>
> *Glenville Kleiser*

And perhaps as you sit here in the present, learning from the past and creating your future; one day in the future you will sit in your new present, congratulating yourself on how far you have come, and moving forward yet again to the next new future, taking all your learning with you.

The book is laid out in seven stages, or steps. Steps 1 and 2 focus on the preparatory work and will help you to put in place some solid foundations on which to build your changes. Step 3 is about preparing the ground for change, by clearing up and learning from your past. Step 4 focuses on your current reality, while Step 5 is about planning your future. Steps 6 and 7 are about you going out and taking action.

Although I do suggest you do them in order, if you have specific issues you want to deal with, you can choose to focus on a particular step. Most people find it helpful to skim through the book first, and then work through the exercises that are most relevant to them over a period of 8-10 weeks. This represents the time you would probably be working with a coach and gives you time to assimilate and apply your learning. While it is true that change can happen in an instant, you do need time to become familiar with the tools, to use them, and to reflect on the changes you are making.

At the start of each section you will find a route planner, which explains in more detail what is covered within that section, and a list of exercises, with rough timings for each. These are just a guide though - if you feel you need to spend more time on any exercise, then just do so.

You can find additional tools, tips and worksheets at **www.joycecampbell.co.uk.**

1

COMMIT

ROUTE PLANNER

The start of any journey requires a commitment, so this section of the book aims to help you to commit to taking the actions necessary for change.

It explores why you might want to learn to coach yourself, and outlines the methods used. You will discover the essential elements of a coaching contract and learn some tips which will enable you to coach yourself successfully.

By the end of this chapter, you will have worked on expanding your comfort zone, taken responsibility for your own success, and begun to reflect on what might be holding you back.

EXERCISES IN THIS SECTION

Expanding your comfort zone	60 minutes
Being at cause	30 minutes
Dealing with your gremlins	30 minutes

THE NUTS AND BOLTS: HOW IT ALL WORKS

YOU need to do the work

Just for a minute, think about what you want to get from this book. Do you want it to be just another self-help book sitting on your bookshelf, with only the first two chapters read? I'm guessing not. I'm guessing that when you bought it, you thought 'This time, this time I'll find what I am looking for'. And you will find it, if you do the exercises and the personal reflection. Self-coaching is not complicated, but the benefits don't come from reading about it, they come from doing it.

> *Seize this moment. Whatever you do or dream you can do, begin it. For boldness has magic, power, and genius in it. Begin it now.*
>
> *Johann Wolfgang van Goethe*

YOU are responsible for getting value from this book

I'm going to say something pretty tough to you here. This stuff works. But ONLY if you take responsibility for getting value from it. This is one of the first things I say to my coaching clients. I cannot do the work for you. And to be honest, even if I could, I wouldn't. Because then the end result would be mine, not yours. Think of an athletics coach. Now there is no doubt that athletes rely on their coaches, need them, value them. However, at the end of the day, who is it that gets up at five in the morning to train? Who has no social life because they need

10 hours sleep a night to recuperate? Who spends hours and hours in physiotherapy, having painful injuries dealt with? Who puts in most effort? And who stands on the winner's podium with the medal round their neck? You don't see the coach squashing up there beside them do you? And that's because at the end of the day, the result belongs to the athlete. They did it. They put in the blood, sweat and tears. In return, they get tremendous gains, a huge feeling of achievement, and a fabulous end result. If you do the work in this book, so will you! Worth the effort? You bet!

Some years ago a new gym opened where I live. I went for a visit, and I swear it looked like paradise. Grecian columns, steam rising from the pool, shimmery underwater lighting. I just HAD to join. We were a bit hard-up at the time, and I couldn't really afford it, but I so wanted a membership there. I was convinced that by just walking through those doors, picking up one of the lovely fluffy robes and free (free!!) slippers, I would transform myself into that image of physical perfection that I knew was in there somewhere. So I convinced my husband that it was an investment, and I handed over my direct debit and committed to a year's membership. I went five times in the first week. I was convinced I had found the place for me. The second week I had a bit of a sniffle, and I didn't really fancy getting all out of breath, so I went along twice for a coffee, and once for a swim. The third week I had a lot on at work, and I went once, but stopped half way through the workout as I felt tired. I never went back.

Every month for the next 11 months I ranted when the direct debit payment came out of my account about it being a waste of money and about the gym being no good. You get the picture. So who was responsible for the lack of value? Me. They stuck to their part of the bargain. They made their service available for a year, they even tried to entice me back several times. But I chose (and believe me, I tried to wriggle out of the concept that it was a choice) not to get value from the investment I had made. So you must commit to taking personal responsibility for getting value from this book. This WILL work - the ideas, tools and concepts in this book are well proven. But they will only work if you do them. They do not work by osmosis. They are not going to jump off your bedside table and into your brain when you aren't looking.

I say there are no short cuts, but that's not completely true. What I can offer you is my experience of the tried and tested. I can use my expertise in coaching to give you examples. I can guide you away from pitfalls. I can help you to avoid blind alleys. But at the end of the day, you must do it.

My training business was years in the planning. Although I had been doing one-to-one work for a long time, it was my dream to start training practitioners of NLP, hypnotherapy and coaching. It was probably one of the best planned businesses around.

Every week I identified one more tweak I needed to make to my plans to get them just perfect. I had employed a business coach to help me make what I described to him as the 'final push'. So every week, he asked me how the business was going and I would say tell him it was great, and then start explaining in great detail what the current tweak was that was stopping me launching. After weeks of this, he asked the question yet again, and I gave him my stock answer, and he laughed. He said to me 'Joyce, you are deluding yourself. You don't HAVE a training business. What you have is a crock of dreams. Just get off your backside and DO something'.

I was hurt beyond belief. I was paying this guy, for heaven's sake. He was meant to be on my side. How dare he say I didn't have a business? The first thing I did was check if I could get out of my contract with him. The second was to look at the first line of our coaching agreement. 'Responsibility for change lies with you, the client.' I realised I was continuing to do all the things I had done before I contracted him to help me make the final push. Once I realised that I was choosing not to get value from the coaching, I committed to change, and faced the fact I was choosing to stay stuck in dreamland (mainly because it was safe, and comfortable, and I got to do one of my favourite activities, which is thinking), then the rest was easy. Within four weeks, I was running my first course. So what will it take to get you out of dreamland? What will it take to put YOU into your new life?

Change is possible: pain is optional!

Change has some key components to it:

- ✓ Preparation

- ✓ Resources

- ✓ Action

As you work through this book, I want you to consider the preparation you need to do. And I don't just mean thinking and planning. I mean self exploration, letting go of stuff that no longer serves you, cutting out the dead wood. We'll be working with your old stories and your beliefs. We'll be looking at the messages you give yourself.

Then I will be asking you to think about the resources you have. I'll be asking you to install some pretty powerful new beliefs, to look at your values and your personal mission, and then to set some compelling goals.

Finally I will be asking you to take action. Powerful, consistent and deliberate action, which will move you step by step to where you want to be.

So are you ready to begin?

LET'S GET GOING!

Stopping or starting?

I've coached many people over the years, and the reasons they come for coaching are remarkably similar. Basically, they want to do more or have more of something, or be better at something; or they want to stop doing something. It's dressed up in lots of different ways - but that's what it boils down to – starting or stopping something. And sometimes in the stopping of one thing, they start something else. Helen came to me simply because she wanted to stop smoking, and she wanted hypnosis. It's seldom as simple as that though – because as we explored her reasons for smoking it became clear to Helen that smoking was actually her way of nurturing her deeply held belief that she wasn't good enough. Six months after we started working together, Helen was packing to go on a great adventure, she had a six month sabbatical from her midwifery post, and she had a round the world air ticket in her hand. Oh – and in case you are wondering, she had stopped smoking as well!

So how does it work?

People often ask me if coaching is the same as therapy. Many coaches will answer that question along the lines that coaching is future and goal focused and therapy is about dealing with the past. Although that's a simple explanation of the differences, I think it does a disservice to the nature of human relationships, and the richness and complexity of our lives.

How I view it is that what happened to you in the past influences your present and your future. The past provides you with a set of lenses or filters through which you view the world. Those filters will lead to the decisions you make about the future. The past also has many resources – tough times in the past will have taught you resilience and strength. They will also have given you some coping mechanisms. Some of these will be good, others may no longer serve you, yet you continue to run them out of habit. It may serve you better now to learn some different strategies.

What you won't be doing is wallowing in the past, re-telling it again and again, re-living and re-imprinting your stories. As a coach, what I like to do is help people clean up their past. It's a bit like de-cluttering your wardrobe using the 'three-pile' method.

The first pile is things which are useful, and which you are going to keep. However, items in this pile need to be checked carefully for broken zips and buttons; sagging hems; smelly armpits. They may need a little maintenance, but overall you are planning to keep them, as they are still useful to you.

The second pile is stuff that no longer serves you - it may have done so once, but you are a different person from the one who bought that stuff initially. Some of it was never truly you, but you ended up hanging onto it as you'd made an investment in it. Some may have suited the person you were once, but you've moved on from that.

And the third pile is stuff that you just love. It has no obvious use, but having it nurtures you in some way. You need to be careful what gets into that pile though. Those size 8 jeans that you are going to fit into again one day may not actually be as useful as you think if they make you miserable every time you look at them. But your baby's first cardigan, still with that unique baby smell, may well be something that it gives you pleasure to have. But it doesn't need to be kicking about every day – you can create a special place to keep those special things.

Once you have sorted out and thrown stuff away, you can see clearly what you currently have, identify the gaps, and plan to fill them.

So as you and I visit your past together through the course of this book, it will be with a purpose of creating order, choosing what to let go, and deciding what to keep as a resource for you in the future.

For me, coaching is more about education than therapy. I'm less interested in why you do something, than in how you do it. My aim is to teach you some skills which will help you understand what (from the past) is still driving you, either consciously or unconsciously, so you can learn what you need to learn, and let it go; to help you assess your current situation in the light of that knowledge and understanding; and to plan effectively for your future. I work from the premise that you aren't broken, and you don't need an expert to 'fix' you. You are a capable person, and you can make all the changes you need for yourself – you may just need someone to show you how to do it. My goal is to give you some tools that will enable you to be fully in charge of your own life.

Imagine being given an operating manual for life. How handy would it be to have one of those at the outset? But we don't have one, and human life and relationships can be messy – sometimes great, sometimes less so. By learning and using the techniques in this book you will be equipped to coach yourself – giving you more of the great, and less of the other. How fantastic would that be? That has to be something worth working for.

BECOME THE COACH YOU DESERVE

Making a contract with yourself

> *Nothing is particularly difficult if you break it into small jobs.*
>
> Henry Ford

When people come to me for coaching, the first thing I do with them is to establish a coaching agreement or contract. We talk about what we can expect from each other, we both commit to the process, and my client tells me the kind of coach they want me to be. Usually what they want from me is three things:

- ✓ Support – a sort of cheerleading role

- ✓ Challenge – not to let them get away with stuff

- ✓ Commitment

They also want the benefit of my understanding about what makes us tick. Now that one is easy – that's the purpose of this book. Unfortunately I can't be there with you to offer you all the rest, but I'm going to ask you to do something even more important. As these things are so crucial to successful coaching, then I'm going to ask you to make a contract with yourself. It has several elements.

Be curious

I got into this line of work because I'm an intensely curious person (some might even say nosey). How people tick has fascinated me since I was a little girl. Milton Erickson, one of the greatest hypnotherapists the world has ever known, was so curious about the changes his clients might make that he was always trying new things. He believed that people were totally capable of change, and he was curious about how they might do it. Imagine being that curious about yourself and about how quickly and easily you will be able to change as you do the exercises in this book. Because this stuff does work, you know. All you have to do is to do it, and be curious about how you will feel when you have changed. What you will hear. What you will see. Curious about the bright new future which is already out there, waiting for you.

Get it in the muscle!

I would also encourage you to start a journal. I can't emphasise how important this is. This journal is going to be crucial for your coaching in the next few weeks. Some of my clients like to buy a special notebook for this purpose: anything from a school-type jotter to a gorgeous bound journal is fine. Others like to use a ring binder, so they can add additional worksheets. Some people open a folder on their computer, and others prefer to set up a blog. Whatever works for you is perfect – the point is that it needs to be in a format you will use.

On a daily basis, I'd like you to write down four key things in your journal. You can use columns, lists, mind-maps or whatever you prefer. This activity is based on a technique called *Temperature Reading*, developed by the family therapist Virginia Satir. I use this exercise at the beginning of every coaching session, and I use it myself at the end of every day. Its purpose is to begin to help you move from problem-based thinking to solution-focused thinking.

The four things I'd like you to write down are:

- ✓ The good things that have happened to you that day

- ✓ Problems you have with possible solutions

- ✓ Any puzzles that are bothering or confusing you

- ✓ Any new information you have about how or what you want to do

Let's look at these in more detail.

Good things that happened to you today

 This part of the exercise is about helping you to filter for the good things in life (more about filters later). It's not always easy, as I found a few weeks ago. I was having a really trying week, and I thought this was going to be an impossible task for me, but when I focused on finding good things, I could find them – the train had run on time; my daughter had chatted to me for an hour (a VERY good thing when they are 14!); and I had got my nail varnish on without smudging. OK, it was shallow, but it made me happy. Other times it will be easy to find good things. But easy or not, I want you to commit to yourself that at the end of every day you find at least six things you appreciate about the day you've just had.

Problems you have together with possible solutions

Yes, you've guessed, it's the second part of this task that is the really important bit. We are very good at focusing on our problems. All the things that didn't go well for us, how rotten we feel, how scared we are. You may have been focused on your problems for weeks, months or years, and yet somehow you haven't solved them yet. Action tends to follow thought. If you look for solutions, you will find them. And you will start to filter things differently, looking for them. Now, note I said 'possible' solutions. They don't have to be fully formed, worked up answers – but unless you can find a possible solution of sorts, the problem becomes larger and more powerful. So even if you can't find a perfect answer, come up with some possibilities. If it is important enough to warrant a place in your journal, it's certainly important enough to have you put some energy into finding a solution.

Puzzles that are bothering or confusing you

This is about recording any puzzles you've come across during the day, and decide how you are going to get the information to solve them. It's OK not to know things. What's not OK is not to make the effort to fill the gaps if you need information to help you to change. An example of this might be that you are currently a stone overweight, and want to run a marathon. You might need information about starting a safe exercise programme, about the kind of shoes you need, or about your diet.

New information

The final thing to write in your journal is any new information you learned today. It might be something you learned as you were doing the exercises; it might be a new skill or technique. It's important to get new learning 'in the muscle' as soon as possible, and one way of doing this is to record it straight away.

Helen, the client who came for hypnosis to stop smoking learned something very important about her beliefs about herself, which she recorded in her journal. Alternatively, it might be something like a new relaxation technique you learned, which you want to practice, or some feedback you received.

A personal example: finding solutions

Let me give you an example of how this worked for me. When I decided to write this book, I had a problem in that I had never written a self-help book before. I was used to writing academic papers, but I had no idea how to write a book. That was my problem. I wrote it down, and thought up lots of possible solutions. The one that seemed most sensible to me was to find someone who had already written a book, so that I could ask them what process they had used. I told all my friends what I wanted. I put it on my blog and in my newsletter. I left online reviews for books that I had enjoyed, in the hope that the author would get in touch. Basically, I started to filter for what I wanted. What actually happened was that one of the authors I had left a review for contacted me to thank me for the feedback I had left her. It turned out she now owned a small publishing company. We had a chat to discuss the potential for working together, and she gave me some advice about how she had created in her imagination what her reader would be like, and wrote her book for them. I was so excited I came off the phone and wrote 5000 words within a few hours. I had it all in me - I just needed someone to give me a clue about how to get it out. That's how powerful this process can be. So please, start your journal now, and commit to doing this exercise every night.

Feather beds are bad for your back: get out of your comfort zone

We all have a comfort zone. That place where we aren't over stretched, where we feel comfortable, and safe. The problem though with comfort zones is that we sometimes don't realise how constricting they are until it's too late. A common metaphor to illustrate this is that if a frog is dropped into almost boiling water, it will jump out immediately. It recognises that it isn't safe, and it takes immediate and irrevocable action to save itself. But if the frog is put into cool water, which is gradually heated up, it becomes slow and soporific and will not move. While biologists have apparently disproved this, like any metaphor or fable, we can learn from it.

Case study: a shrinking comfort zone

One of the very first clients I had, nearly 30 years ago, was Marion. Marion was a young woman who had been recently bereaved. One day not long after the funeral she was shopping in a big supermarket. She was tired, she hadn't eaten much, and the store was crowded and hot. While standing at the checkout she suddenly had a panic attack. Panic attacks are horrible when they happen, and Marion had been so frightened, she thought she was dying. She also believed she'd made a fool of herself by crying, sobbing and pushing past people to get to the exit. Two days later she went back to the same shop and had the thought 'what if it happens again?' As she remembered the frightening sensations of her last attack, her body produced the sensations again (remember, action follows thought), and she had a second attack. She decided that in future she would use a smaller shop nearer home. However, as she entered the smaller store, she talked to herself again about her previous attacks, building up what is called in NLP a *sensory rich experience*. That is, she created a picture, with sounds and feelings, of an attack. She quickly produced a third panic attack. Within six weeks of her first attack Marion had made her comfort envelope so small that she would not leave the house. She called me the day she realised that she was working out how feasible it would be to put a small make-shift kitchen and a commode into the corner of her living room so she did not have to leave the one room when she was in the house by herself.

With all the tools of hypnosis, time code interventions and NLP that I have at my fingertips nowadays I could probably help Marion much quicker than I could then, but I can say that it took much longer to expand the envelope again than it had taken for it to contract. But Marion did challenge herself, and in time was able to live a normal life again.

> *The lust for comfort, that stealthy thing that enters the house as a guest, and then becomes a host, and then a master.*
>
> *Kahlil Gibran*

What had happened was that initially Marion had used avoidance techniques and her comfort zone shrank rapidly. I'm sure that you can think of times where you have let your comfort zone shrink until it's more like a strait-jacket than a cocoon. It's no longer simply keeping you safe, but actually stifling and limiting you. Let's explore this further.

Think of your comfort zone as a shape, for example, a circle. Inside the circle is the stuff which is easy and comfortable for you, and stuff you feel safe doing. Outside the circle is risk: new things, things that scare you, areas where you may not yet have much skill. The actual circumference of the circle is the boundary between those two places. Now you have a choice. You can either push on that boundary, taking tiny little baby-steps if necessary, to nudge the circle slightly bigger, or you can avoid going too near the edge 'just in case' and the consequence of that is that the boundary will actually shrink. Which option will you choose? Take some time now to do the following exercise.

> *When you can no longer change the world, you are challenged to change yourself.*
>
> *Viktor Frankl*

Exercise: expanding your comfort zone

This exercise is going to help you expand your comfort zone, by exploring where the boundaries currently sit, and identifying what you would like to have within a new expanded comfort zone.

✓ Get a large piece of paper and some coloured pens. Stick a photograph of yourself right in the middle of the paper. Think about everything you feel confident, comfortable or safe about doing. Write them on the paper, next to your photograph – the more relaxed and comfortable you feel about them, the nearer they should go to your photo. You can take a 'whole life' view of this, or if you prefer, focus on one context, such as work or relationships.

✓ Once you've done that, take a different coloured pen, and draw a rough oval or circle which encloses all the things you have just written down. This is your comfort zone. Now, just think about it – there was a time when everything in this zone was also a bit of an unknown, but you learned to do everything here – perhaps by taking some risks, perhaps through practice, perhaps through challenging yourself, perhaps by copying or modelling other people. One way or another, you learned to do these things, and they are now easy and comfortable to you.

✓ After you have completed your comfort map move onto the next stage. Make a list of things you would like to do. Remember, these are things YOU want to do, so don't write this list to please other people. It doesn't matter if you have sky-diving or 'say hello to the nice guy I see on the train every morning'. It's yours – put on it the things YOU want but currently aren't doing. Once you have your list, write them in the map, outside your comfort zone circle, again putting the easier (to you) things nearest you, and the harder things further away. This is your possibility zone. Have a good look at your possibility zone. Acknowledge that there is probably stuff that you haven't even allowed on the paper, just in case I suggest that you do them! Relax about these for now. Also, forget for now all the things that are right at the edge of the paper. In

> *'Come to the edge',*
> *he said. They said,*
> *'We are afraid'.*
> *'Come to the edge',*
> *he said. They came.*
> *He pushed them...*
> *and they flew.*
>
> *Guillaume Apollinaire*

Step 5, you'll be ready to come back to them – I promise you!

✓ For now, look at the thing that is nearest the outside edge of your comfort zone – maybe even sitting right on the boundary. Have a think about what it will look like when you've done that. How pleased will you be with yourself? What is the first step that would take you there? What is the second?

✓ Take a deep breath, and start working towards that one thing. Remember, it's nearly in your comfort zone already, so all you need to do is expand that boundary a little bit. Once you feel ready, start picking off things one at a time, until one day in the not too distant future, you will realise that everything currently in your possibility zone has moved into your expanded comfort zone, and your possibility zone is full of.....well.....new possibilities!

You might be wondering what you should do if you notice some resistance to moving out of your comfort zone. You might be saying things like 'what will people think of me' or 'it will be so embarrassing if I mess up' or 'I'm too shy/old/fat to do that' or 'I might lose my friends'. Being bold enough to push back the boundaries of your comfort zone does not mean you won't feel fear. It means that despite the fear, you do it anyway. So if you notice avoidance, simply acknowledge that you are afraid, and then DO IT ANYWAY.

On page 24 you will see a possibility map drawn by one of my clients, Mark, who was finding it very difficult to be assertive at work.

Figure 1: Mark's possibility map

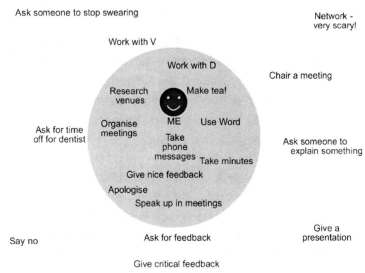

Mark decided that he would start pushing his comfort zone outwards by initially offering to work with a colleague, Victoria, who in the past he had found to be intimidating. He was surprised when she welcomed his input and that gave him confidence to ask his manager for feedback on his performance. Unfortunately, his manager wasn't particularly skilled in this area, and gave a lot of subjective feedback which Mark found hard to hear. Nevertheless, after we debriefed this in coaching, Mark realised that some of it did have some basis in fact, and he felt able to go back to his manager and ask for his input on how he could improve his performance. Within two weeks of starting the process, Mark had pushed right to the edge of his possibility zone, and he had new things to put in it. He now feels ready to apply for more senior positions. What could you achieve if you pushed to the edge of your comfort zone?

Often we try to stay in our comfort zone even when it's not safe or appropriate to do so. Some years ago I was learning to ski. Again and again the instructor told me that as I crossed the slope, my weight should be on my downhill ski. That instruction was totally counter intuitive and very frightening – to do it required me to lean away from the side of the hill, and out into the open. Again and again I resisted his instruction. Consciously I was willing and understood, but my unconscious mind repeatedly told me it was too scary and dangerous, and tried to pull me back into the side of the hill. Other people passed through the class and moved up to the next level, and I was stuck in the beginners' class, unable to move on. The irony was that the more I leaned into the side of the hill, the more I fell. The very thing that seemed to be keeping me safe was causing me to be hurt and embarrassed, and was holding me back from progressing. In the end I had to act on trust – I simply had to believe that no matter how safe it felt to lean into the mountain, I was never going to ski until I stood up and leaned away from the slope. Within minutes of doing that, I made my first successful descent. Sometimes in order to move out of our comfort zone, we need to take the big leap of faith that we can survive whatever lies out there. Resisting what makes you feel uncomfortable can actually be the worst possible thing to do.

Be at cause

One of the hardest and most important concepts I am going to ask you to take on is about taking responsibility for what happens to you. In NLP terms, this is called being *at cause*. Being at cause is often confused with being at fault. This is not about blame - but it IS about responsibility.

Case study: taking responsibility

Elaine is someone I found completely inspirational with regard to this concept. Over the period of a few years, she had run up literally tens of thousands of credit card debt. Initially, she thought she could get out of the situation by further borrowing to consolidate her loans, and she applied for every credit card offer that came through her door – and five years ago, there were lots on offer. Of course, she could barely cover the minimum payment, so crippling interest rates meant the debt rapidly mounted up. The day it topped £65000 all credit suddenly ran dry. She stood in the supermarket offering one card after another, and they were all refused. After months of burying her head in the sand, and evading calls from debt collectors, Elaine suddenly went to cause.

At a time when others were blaming the banks for over-lending, Elaine took full responsibility for the decisions she had made. With the help of a debt-management agency, she drew up a detailed budget, and negotiated a repayment plan. Overnight she changed her life: clothes for the entire family now came from charity shops; children's toys from car boot sales. She learned to cook from scratch, and eventually got an allotment and learned to hatch chickens so that the family could become more self-sufficient.

Five years on, the debt management agency views her as a success story, as she has not once defaulted on a re-payment, and has not taken on any more debt. Holidays are now taken off-season in a tent, at low cost campsites. At the current rate, she won't be debt-free for another 30 years, but I have never once heard her moan or complain.

Her children have everything they need, and have a keen awareness of value for money, saving for what you want, and caring for the environment. Elaine herself is optimistic and humorous, and great fun to be around. Her solutions would not necessarily be yours, but the interesting thing for me was that while she continued to place responsibility outside herself - everyone was borrowing too much; the banks pushed credit on people who couldn't really afford to re-pay it - then her debt continued to rise. The minute she said 'I chose to get into this mess, now I have to get out of it', everything changed.

By accepting responsibility for having made choices which have brought you to where you currently are in your life, you reach a point where you are able to move on, rather than adopting a 'why me' attitude.

I can recognise when my clients are not at cause by the language they use. It usually involves putting the responsibility outside themselves, having lots of excuses about why they can't change, and saying 'yes, but...' a lot! Sometimes tough things do happen to us in life, but we have choices about how we deal with them. When we accept that, we can move on much more quickly and effectively.

If as you read this, you are getting annoyed, and coming up with lots of exceptions to the need to be at cause, then I can tell you, you probably aren't! That is your choice. It's not my job or anyone else's to drag you kicking and screaming to cause if you don't want to be there. What I would say though, is that no one can change until they are at cause, because until that point they have not taken responsibility for whatever situation they are in, and for how to get out of it.

I know this isn't always easy. I'm certainly not perfect in this area – sometimes I like a good whine as much as the next person. But even when I'm doing that, I acknowledge to myself that's exactly what I am doing. I'm doing 'poor me' to get some sympathy, or attention, or to get out of doing something I don't want to do. But while I'm doing 'poor me' I can't change, I just keep going over old ground. So my challenge to you, as your coach, is to pay attention to those times when you are not at cause, and do what you need to do in order to be there. And if you don't want to, then acknowledge that you are choosing not to change.

Exercise: being at cause

This exercise will help you explore the areas in your own life where you may not yet be totally at cause.

- ✓ Make a list of all the excuses you have for not changing

- ✓ Now look at the list carefully. How many of them are really things you could get round if you wanted to? How many of them could you simply ignore? How many of them might change anyway if you just got going?

Eliminating the gremlins

What are you not doing that you could be doing? What is it that's stopping you? For most people it's limiting beliefs that have been internalised over the years. They might be beliefs about the world being dangerous, about us not being capable, or about not being good enough. These little gremlins hold us back. Our gremlins are the parts of ourselves that attempt to sabotage change. They tell us that things are too hard, too scary, too difficult, and not for us. They say things like 'Why take the risk?' and 'If it ain't broke, don't fix it'. They constantly seek to return us to the old status quo.

Exercise: dealing with your gremlins

Part of being an effective coach is to help clients identify when their gremlin is speaking. You are going to work on tackling and identifying your own gremlins. Sometimes it's enough to simply ask the question of 'Who is saying that?'Some people find it helpful to personify their gremlin in some way. You can ask:

- ✓ 'If my gremlin had a name, what would it be?'

- ✓ 'What is my gremlin fond of saying to me?'

- ✓ 'What are the favourite gremlin comments in my family'?

Write your responses in your journal.

One of the important skills of self-coaching is to be able to recognise how you sabotage yourself, and what your gremlins are. Once you find them, you can either politely ask them to go, and tell them they have no place in your life now – or you can squash them flat!

Case study: silencing the gremlin

Jennifer had a gremlin that talked to her in her mother's voice. It said things like 'Don't rock the boat', 'It's a jungle out there', and 'If anything happens to you I couldn't bear it.' Jennifer had a dream to move to set up her own business. She loathed her job as an office administrator, and wanted to set up an ironing business. She also loved her mum, and didn't want to do anything destructive to the voice. So she imagined that her mother was sitting beside her, and told her 'Mum, I know you love me, and I love you, and I really appreciate how you've cared for me. I'm going to go for this business opportunity, but I want you to know I've thought it through really carefully and I'm going to grow the business gradually without taking on a lot of debt.' She practised saying that assertively and with love, until she felt able to say it to her mum – who, when faced with Jennifer's sense of confidence and surety, put up much less argument than Jennifer had expected.

How committed are you, really?

Finally, let's talk about commitment. Clients nearly always say this is important to them in the coaching contract. What they want is for me to feel 100 per cent committed to them, and to their success. So I want you to ask yourself how committed you are to this process. And I mean really committed. Not just in a 'glance through the book' way, but how committed are you to actually doing the exercises, keeping your journal, and moving forwards?

Give yourself a score from one to ten. Anything less than eight and my guess is that you are still not fully at cause, and have not accepted responsibility for the changes you want to make. What do you need to do to make your level of commitment a ten? Because if it's not up there now, when you are at the very start of the process, how are you going to maintain it when the going gets tough? If this is important to you, you need to commit to it, now.

CHECKPOINT

Once you've completed the exercises in this section, you will have a robust coaching contract with yourself, and be ready to truly be the coach you deserve. Here's what you should have achieved.

- ✓ Committed to being curious

- ✓ Started a journal

- ✓ Drawn your comfort zone and possibility map

- ✓ Considered the concept of being at cause, and be ready to accept responsibility for change

- ✓ Identified your gremlins

- ✓ Assessed your level of commitment, and raised it to a 10

Give yourself a huge message of appreciation for your commitment so far, and when you are ready let's move on to building your support system.

2

DEVELOP YOUR
SUPPORT SYSTEM

ROUTE PLANNER

Support is a key element to successful change. Wouldn't it be useful if you could learn strategies which would enable you to be your own support system, while at the same time being able to work creatively with other people?

In this section you will learn to do both of these, while also exploring how in the past you may have sabotaged yourself.

By the end of the section, you'll have had a chance to develop your own inner cheerleader, pulled together a Board of Advisors, and identified what you need in terms of real-life support.

EXERCISES IN THIS SECTION

Changing the soundtrack	15 minutes
Being good to yourself	60 minutes
Your Board of Advisors	30 minutes

YOU'RE GOOD!

Nearly everyone who comes for coaching wants support in one form or another. Now as I'm not going to be there to provide that for you, you need to work on developing your own support system.

Making friends with your inner cheerleader

Let's think about support for a moment. What does that look like to you? What does it sound like? What does it feel like to know you are supported? What would it be like to build that support internally, so that it's always there?

I wonder if you have one of these little voices in your head? That voice is your self-talk, and it keeps up a running commentary. I used to have a voice that said things like 'Who do you think you are, teaching people this stuff?', 'What makes you so special?' On a bad day, it would get really insulting 'You're so thick. You'll never do this.' Even years after I thought I had dealt with that voice, there it was one day, back in full force when I had my first attempt at writing this book. 'You'll never do it. Fifty THOUSAND words? Who are you kidding?' Yet here you are, holding the book in your hands, evidence that I somehow turned my voice off and got on with it, and you can too. Even better than turning it off, my voice now says much more empowering and supportive things to me. Just imagine for a moment what it would be like to have a voice that said to you 'You're doing brilliantly. You're brave/smart/funny/clever. You can do this. I'm so proud of you.' Feels good, doesn't it?

Someone said to me once that they thought it was a bit delusional to be saying all these nice things to yourself. My response to that would be that it is certainly no more delusional than telling yourself all day long that you are rubbish! And anyway, energy and action follow thought, so surely it's better to be saying great things, then getting great results, therefore proving yourself right; than it is to be saying horrible things, getting poor results, and proving yourself right? Because actually you will – whatever you think about yourself you will produce.

Case study: getting to great!

Susan had a voice that constantly said 'You're rubbish'. The voice was so powerful, that Susan actually went to some effort to ensure it was given full voice. If you asked how she was, she'd say rubbish. If you asked how her holiday was, she'd say rubbish. She described herself as a rubbish mother, with a rubbish job. When I pointed out to her how often she said it, she was initially fairly defensive – how could a single word have so much power, it was just a habit. So I challenged her to change the habit, and replace rubbish with the word 'great' for a week: both externally and internally. I helped by sending her a text every morning saying 'it's a great day, you're a great person, go out and have a great time!' Susan reported that while she'd been sceptical in the extreme, after a week of telling herself everything was great, she felt better equipped to deal with what were some very real challenges in her life. What have you got to lose?

Exercise: changing the soundtrack

This exercise is designed to help you change the soundtrack forever. Just sit quietly, and really pay attention to that internal voice. What tone does it use? What is the volume like? Is it harsh or soft? Does it remind you of anyone? Ask yourself if you would speak to another person in this way. Now, what I want you to do is to start playing around with this voice. If it helps, imagine that you have your own voice software, which you can manipulate electronically. As you make each change, notice if it makes the voice more or less pleasant. Turn the volume up, or down. Make it soft.... harsh..... crisp. Move it far away from you, and then up close in your ear. Pay attention to what makes a difference. Now have it say something really lovely to you. If it's easier, imagine that you are saying it to someone else, or to a much younger version of you. Now the next time that old voice bothers you, I want you to immediately change it, so that it has all the elements of that nicer voice, and have it say something pleasant.

The purpose of this exercise is to develop that internal cheerleader to a degree that the instant that old voice shows up, you just go 'Uh, uh, there's that old voice', and immediately change it to the new improved version. At the end of the day, would you rather live with old grumpy drawers, who nags you and puts you down all the time, or would you rather live with someone who thought you were pretty damn special? I know which I would choose. And the choice is yours. By choosing to beat yourself up all the time (and it IS a choice, no matter how hard that is to accept) then you choose to keep yourself stuck.

Choosing to keep yourself stuck is an unpalatable truth, and I know it's one I struggled with a lot. I was furious with my first coach, an amazing old man who was my very first hypnosis teacher, when he asked me when I was going to be ready to let go of being stuck. I raged and fumed. I insisted that he had no idea about the terrible time I'd had. He could not seriously think

I was choosing this. Yada, yada. But as I worked with him, I realised that my voice was keeping me nice and safe. It stopped me from taking risks, and it stopped me from trying new things. And if I didn't try, well, then I couldn't fail. I could blame everything on everyone else.

So the single most important form of support you can give yourself is to learn to be your own cheerleader. Deal with the voice.

Look after the goose: one roast dinner or eggs for life?

Next, do whatever you need to do to nurture yourself. Have you ever been on a plane? Remember how in the safety briefing you are told to put your own oxygen mask on before helping others? There's a reason for that – you can't help others if you are dead! It's the same in life – if you run yourself into the ground in some sort of martyrdom, then you won't be able to give your kids, your partner, or your work the attention they deserve and need longer term. So it's not selfish to pay attention to your own needs, it's essential. Do you know the story of the goose and the golden eggs? The farmer was amazed and delighted to acquire a goose that laid a golden egg every day. So much so, that eventually he couldn't wait for the daily egg, so he killed the goose in order to get at all the eggs quickly. But of course, there were no more eggs – the goose only had the capacity to make one egg a day. So it is with you – kill the goose, and the best you can hope for is one nice roast dinner. But there will be no more eggs.

Exercise: being good to yourself

This exercise is to help you identify, and commit to, ways of looking after yourself.

Use Table 1 on page 42 to make a list of 10 things that you could do on a weekly basis that would help nurture and sustain you. I suggest you have a range of things covering physical, emotional/spiritual and mental. Do it now. Because this stuff works IF you do it. Reading about it isn't enough. So make your list either in the table or in your journal.

Now you are going to assess your level of commitment. Looking at your list, on a score of 1-10, how committed do you feel to doing them? More than seven? Then that's really excellent. What do you have to do to lift it right up to 10? Perhaps see yourself at the end of the week looking so much better, fresher and brighter, having achieved that first step to a new you. Or perhaps just feel the sense of relaxation and pride that you will have when you've looked after yourself. Or perhaps you might hear yourself saying 'well done' and maybe other people are telling you that you look well. Are you there yet? Do whatever it takes to get to a 10, and then start doing them.

What if your motivation is less than seven? The first thing to do in that case is to go back and check if they really are things that light your fire. We are bombarded with health promotion messages nowadays, so maybe the things you've chosen are what you feel you SHOULD do, rather than things you really want to do. There is no point having a five mile run on your list if the thought of doing it fills you with dread. This is not an endurance test – you should only have on the list things that really will make you feel better while you do them.

Alternatively, maybe you are a stick person rather than a carrot person. In NLP we describe this as someone with an 'away from' motivation strategy (carrot people have a towards motivation strategy). In that case, you won't be motivated by how good you will feel after you've made the changes. But you might be motivated to consider how bad you will feel if you don't. Just imagine, for a moment, another week, another month, another year, of doing what you've been doing. Getting more and more stuck. That voice getting louder and more insistent. What will happen if you don't change? What will you be like in a year's time if you keep on doing the same old stuff? Just do it now – imagine your life is a film, and run it forwards a year. Another year of not changing. Of doing exactly what you've been doing. Just notice what you look like – do you look refreshed and energised? Or tired, drawn and exhausted? How are you feeling? Full of beans, happy, relaxed? Or stressed, anxious, worn out? Maybe people are saying 'So and so has aged a lot recently, hasn't she?' Just notice whatever you need to notice in order to get that motivation cranked up to a 10.

Once you've completed the table, the next step is to schedule these things into your plans for the coming week. No excuses now - because these aren't my ideas, they are the things you've identified as important for you. If you need to drop something else to make room for them, then get that organised. If you need to get up a bit earlier, then commit to doing so. Get it in your diary, or on your planner, or in your online calendar: where ever you plan your week. If you aren't in the habit of planning things, you may want to re-think that.

Some people worry that if they schedule in 'me-time' activities they will lose the chance to be spontaneous. My response to that is by not scheduling in time for ourselves we risk never actually getting any, as we will always be reacting to what is going on around us.

Now do it. Go and do the first thing you are going to do to nurture and support yourself, and then come back, refreshed and ready to carry on.

Table 1: being good to yourself

What am I going to do?	When will I do it?	Commitment level (1-10)
1.		
2.		
3.		
4.		
5.		
6.		
7.		
8.		
9.		
10.		

Board of Advisors

Imagine what it would be like if you had access to some of the most creative, inspiring people in the world, and that you could call upon them to advise you. Some years ago now I read an amazing book called *Think and Grow Rich* by Napoleon Hill. In it, Hill talks about how he refined his own character by modelling himself on nine people who he particularly admired. Over a period of many years, he held regular imaginary council meetings with these people, who he called his invisible counsellors. He would simply shut his eyes, and imagine that his counsellors were sitting around a table with him.

The next exercise is to help you create your own Board of Advisors. As it involves you doing some visualisation, I suggest you read through it carefully before you begin. A quick word here about visualisations - people sometimes say to me that they can't visualise. I think the problem is that they are often expecting to produce mental pictures as sharp as if they were taken with a top of the range camera. It won't necessarily be like that for you. But think for a moment of your front door, or your car if you have one. What colour is it? Now in order to answer that question, you had to make a picture. That's all visualising is. Everyone can do it, some people simply do it so quickly that they aren't aware of it consciously. In order to do this exercise effectively, you need to let go of the concept of 'trying', a concept which in itself implies the potential of failure. Relax and go with the flow, and notice what happens.

Exercise: creating your Board of Advisors

Creating your personal Board of Advisors has several steps:

- ✓ First of all, jot down a list of no more than 10 people that you would like to get advice from. It's often easier to start with three or four, and add to them over time. Chose anyone you want. They can be people you actually know in real life: friends, relatives, colleagues; or they can be people from history or business; or they can be celebrities. They can be dead or alive. The important thing is that you really rate their skills in an area you want to work on, you respect them, and you would want to act on any advice they gave you. Personally, I find it helpful to have people who would have different perspectives. So I have on my board someone with a sound no-nonsense business head, and also someone who brings a more spiritual perspective.

- ✓ Once you have your list, find a quiet place where you won't be disturbed for 15 minutes. Make yourself comfortable, close your eyes, and take a few deep breaths, in through your nose and out through your mouth, until you feel relaxed.

- ✓ Imagine a table – it can be your own dining room or kitchen table, or it can be a formal boardroom table. Use whatever comes. Ensure that in your imagination, the table has chairs round it, with one at the head for you. Place all your advisors around you.

✓ Tell your advisors the challenge you want help with. Imagine yourself actually saying it to them. Ask them for their suggestions.

✓ Simply wait and listen. Let your mind go empty. You might get a feeling as to what the answer is, you may hear yourself say it, or it may seem as if your advisor actually says it. You may even get a picture. When you have a sense of having received an answer, thank your advisors, and leave the room.

✓ When you are ready, open your eyes and come back to the present. You might find it helpful to write your learning from this exercise in your journal.

This is an exercise that gets easier every time you do it. You can return to your Board again and again in the future and ask for their support with any questions. Here are some of the things my clients have said that they asked their advisors:

✓ What is my true purpose in life?

✓ How can I best express that?

✓ What can I do, right now, that will move me forwards?

✓ What beliefs do I need to let go of?

✓ What is the single most important piece of advice you can give me?

No doubt you will have more questions of your own to add to this list. This really does work – try it for yourself, play about with it, and have some fun bringing lots of new support to your team.

Building your dream-team

The final part of your support team is the real life people you have around you. One of the hardest things you might encounter if you are making positive changes in your life is friends and family who are always trying to drag you back to the old status quo. If you are getting fit and healthy, they may say things like 'You've lost enough weight now' (when you are still three stone from target) or 'One cake won't hurt'. They might say you're no fun anymore; or they might try to put you back in your place with teasing about getting above yourself.

> *Keep away from people who try to belittle your ambitions. Small people always do that, but the really great ones make you feel as if you too, can become great.*
>
> *Mark Twain*

Take a good look at the people in your life right now. Are they positive and enthusiastic? Do you feel energised by being with them? Do they want you to succeed, and are they supportive of what you want in life? Or do you feel a bit stuck, and dragged down when you are with them? Does your energy just seep away after an hour in their company? If so, you might want to ask yourself if being around people who are holding you back and dragging you down is really in your best interests. Have you just become comfortable with their negativity? I'm not saying here that you shouldn't be there for a friend going through a bad patch. If someone is bereaved, or going through a bad relationship, or worried about their health, then of course we will want to help. Likewise, friends can often offer us a different perspective on an issue, or suggest some refinements to a plan. This fly-on-the-wall feedback can be incredibly useful, so I certainly don't mean that you should cut people out of your life simply because they don't agree with you. These comments are offered with your best interests at heart, and you can choose to accept or reject them. But what if this is a long term suck-you-dry relationship?

In that case, you might have some tough decisions to make. You might feel that the relationship is still worth investing in, in which case you might want to put your energies into showing them some options. You might want to reduce your contact with them, or you might even decide it's time to let them go with love. You will find a useful technique for cutting bonds on page 89.

You might also find it useful to re-read page 21 about expanding your comfort zone, as one of the reasons we often stick around these kinds of people is no more complex than we were friends once – perhaps thrown together by circumstance: we had a baby at the same time; we sat opposite them at work; or they were in the room next to us at university. We've got so used to them that it seems more hassle to drop them than it does to keep them. Plus of course, always the sneaking anxiety of 'Will anyone else actually like me?' Yes, they will!

Start thinking about how or where to find other people who have similar interests to you, and a positive attitude, and start to be around them more. If you are looking to develop some key skills, be with someone who is at least one step further along the way than you, and model what they do. You will soon find that your support team is full of people who want to support you, and see you flourish.

Case study: letting someone go

Craig had been working as an engineer for four years, and was desperately unhappy. He decided that he wanted to retrain as a plumber, and set up his own business. He was able to find an accelerated course which took account of his prior training, and he set up his own business within weeks of qualifying, employing some older and experienced plumbers to plug any gaps in his practical skills. He was puzzled though that his best friend did everything possible to dissuade him. He accused him of selling out. He talked endlessly about how awful it would be to go back to college.

Once his business was established (and with a contract from his old employers to start him off), Craig's friend belittled him, and joked when he saw him at work about being 'the help'. This friend had provided lots of beer-fuelled sessions when they shared stories about how awful their day job was. But Craig had decided to move on, and his friend hadn't. In the end, Craig decided that he had to cut the cords. He still saw his friend now and again, but had no emotional link with him.

You need to ask yourself the question: why would anyone who loves me want me to be unhappy or unhealthy? The answer is that if you change, you will move out of their orbit and influence.

Anything less than support (and I do include a healthy dose of constructive criticism as support) is sabotage. When we change, and our friends don't, then the message that they may take from this is that they are wrong. That can be an uncomfortable place for many people: they are losing the friend who always had a little less money than them; who was never quite as fit as they were; who stayed in the job with them. And if you change, then it proves it can be done – and suddenly they are faced with the fact that they could also change, if they put the effort in. But they aren't prepared to do that, so they sabotage you. Don't let them.

CHECKPOINT

Still with the programme? Excellent!

In this section the focus was on getting all the support in place for you to have the life you want. You should have:

- ✓ Connected with your inner cheerleader, and learned how to adjust that voice inside so that it is telling you how fabulous you are.

- ✓ Identified at least 10 ways of nurturing your body, mind and soul on a regular basis, and planned some time in your diary to do these activities.

- ✓ Built your Board of Advisors.

- ✓ Built your dream-team of real life support.

Additionally, you should now be in the habit of updating your journal every day, and taking regular temperature readings. If you have been doing all the exercises and taking reflection time, then it will have taken you about two weeks to get to this stage. I can't emphasise enough – reading about the exercises isn't sufficient – you need to do them, and connect with what you discover. Please don't rush this process.

Now you have all this in place, we are going to go on and look at clearing out the past.

3

CLEARING THE GROUND

ROUTE PLANNER

Have you ever had the experience of taking over a garden which has been neglected and is overgrown with weeds? Before you can get on with planting and nourishing new growth, you first need to get rid of all the weeds and deadwood that might stop new plants from flourishing. Sometimes during that process you might also find hidden treasures: things that with a little care you can nurse back to vigour.

In the same way we need to prepare ourselves for change. This section of the book works on resolving your past hurts, and at the same time assisting you to find amazing resources and learning from the past, even if it was tough.

By the end of this section you will have learned how to let go of emotions, beliefs and experiences which no longer serve you well, while at the same time installing powerful new beliefs which will support you in the future.

EXERCISES IN THIS SECTION

Tidying up the unconscious mind	20 minutes
Appreciating your inner child	60 minutes
Redrawing your memories	10 minutes
Sorting out your stories	20 minutes
The mind body connection	5 minutes
Do you really believe that?	90 minutes
Becoming aligned	30 minutes
Putting new beliefs in your memory storage system	30 minutes
Cutting the cords that bind you	30 minutes

YOUR UNCONCSIOUS MIND

Do you have a loft or attic in your house? The one in our house is stuffed with things that have accumulated over the years. Up there we have everything from university lecture notes; photographs and vinyl records; baby clothes and toys; books; packaging material; Christmas decorations; pieces of furniture and lots more. Unfortunately, we really have no idea what there is up there – it holds the detritus of nearly 30 years of married life and half a dozen house moves. There may actually be lots of useful stuff there, but we would never find it easily. One day, the aim is to go up there and methodically sort out the lot. One day!

Much of our past is stored in our unconscious mind, and can be a bit like that attic - full of things that might be helpful to us if we could only find them, but also full of things that are simply taking up space, and possibly at some level holding us back.

Your unconscious mind is a pretty amazing thing. It is the place where you store all your memories, your experience, your beliefs, values, and your learning. You have lots of useful things in there – things that if you had to do consciously every time would take a lot of effort. Can you imagine having to think consciously about how to tie your shoe laces?

When you learn anything new, the pattern is to go through a cycle of integrating the learning that eventually leads you to a state of unconscious competence – a state of simply 'just knowing' how to do a thing, without any conscious effort at all. While this is incredibly useful for all sorts of purposes - breathing, walking, driving a car or tying our shoelaces - it also has a down side. When you learn a phobia, for example, you become unconsciously competent at running it, so that every single time you experience the trigger, you run the phobia. If you have a spider phobia, and you see a spider, you don't tend to go, 'Wow, spider. Time to have my phobia. The first thing I need to do is speed my heart rate up. The next thing I need to do is start to sweat.' You just see it, and run the phobia almost instantaneously. In fact, phobias tend to be something that can be learned extremely effectively, and also very quickly. Often only one exposure is necessary in order to learn how to run a phobia perfectly every time. In fact, it's probably easier to learn how to replicate a phobic reaction than it is to learn to tie your shoelaces. Remember Marion, my client with agoraphobia? After only one panic attack in a crowded shop, she was able to produce that same phobic reaction in several different contexts.

So your unconscious mind certainly has enormous potential for learning. And that's why NLP can be great for dealing with problems from the past – if you can learn things quickly, then you can also unlearn them quickly, by replacing them with a new strategy.

Now think for a moment about memories. Have you ever had that experience of smelling something - a certain perfume, aftershave, a flower, even a cooking smell - and being transported straight into the past, to an event that you hadn't thought about for years? I was passing a street-seller making candy floss the other day, and in seconds I was back as a teenager, hanging around the fairground with my friend. I could hear the music, see the waltzers, and actually experience internally all the feelings of excitement I had that night. I could even see what my friend and I were wearing. When I really concentrated, I could actually feel the label inside the yellow dress I was wearing – the one that always gave me a tiny little itchy spot on the back of my neck. So just by following a smell, within seconds I could produce an entire sensory rich experience, with pictures, sounds and feelings, of something I hadn't thought about for decades - and at a conscious level, didn't even realise was still in there. Those of you who are parents may notice that you almost have a spontaneous age regression when you go into your child's school - the sights and smells of a classroom mean you access that experience of childhood again. Or there is the 'our song' phenomenon, where only a few bars of music can instantly transport us to another time.

This is all fine when the memories are good ones, but you might also have memories with emotions such as anger, sadness, fear and guilt attached to them, and if you keep re-accessing those memories, then your reactions may range from using energy to keep stuffing them back under the radar, to running your entire life based on the emotions and beliefs these memories generate in you.

Case study: finding the imprint experience

Tracey had been bullied in her first term of high school. Neither the school nor her parents had been particularly understanding at the time, and no action had been taken to protect her – the attitude was very much that she needed to toughen up and learn to cope. The bullying had lasted for about three months, from September through to Christmas, when the family moved because of her father's job. In particular, every time she spoke in class, a group of girls would start to laugh and snigger. As our unconscious mind works hard to protect us, Tracey had managed to more or less forget the experience consciously. She was now a junior manager in a large multinational company, and at an annual review received feedback that she was perceived as being weak in meetings. Coaching had been suggested to help her work on her assertiveness skills.

As is so often the case though, the surface issue was just a symptom, and not a root cause of the problem. In coaching, Tracey said that every time she was required to speak at a meeting, or in front of a group, she felt enormous anxiety, and had an almost overwhelming desire to remove herself from the situation, but she had no idea what was causing it. I asked her remain safely in her chair beside me, while projecting the imaginary movie of her life onto the wall in front of her, and run it backwards until she found the first time she had experienced the problem. Initially she said she had always been like that, that she had hated tutorial groups at university, and had not been good at speaking up at high school. As she couldn't initially find a trigger, I asked her to run the movie further back to a time when the problem hadn't existed, and her face changed when she realised that at junior school, she had 'always had something to say for herself'. It only took a few minutes of running the movie forward again for Tracey to find the root cause. She said that she'd been at that school for such a short time, she had actually forgotten about it. But her unconscious mind hadn't forgotten, and in an attempt to keep her safe from similar humiliation, had effectively ensured that she kept silent in group situations. Tracey didn't need assertiveness skills training, what she needed was support in resolving the hurt done to her as a child, to take any learning she needed from the experience, and to let the rest of it go.

TECHNIQUES FOR RESOLUTION

Getting out the rose-tinted glasses: visualisation for change

One of the nicest and easiest ways to start tidying up the unconscious mind is by using hypnosis. The unconscious mind likes stories and metaphor and responds very well to visualisation techniques. Read through the visualisation exercise below a couple of times till you get the key points, and then practice it – you don't need to memorise it – if you have the general flow, your unconscious mind will fill in the detail for you.

You can also record it, and play it to yourself. If you do this, record it in a slow and gentle voice, with lots of pauses. It should take you around 20 minutes to do this exercise, and you can return to it many times.

Exercise: tidying up the unconscious mind

Find a quiet spot where you won't be disturbed. If it helps, put some relaxing music on. Tell yourself that you are going to do some visualisation, and that if you need to at any point you can return to full awareness by simply opening your eyes. Make yourself comfortable, and close your eyes. Take a few slow deep breaths. Scan your body for any signs of stress or tension, and let your muscles relax.

Imagine you are sitting on a really comfortable chair, watching a screen in front of you. Let an image of an attic appear on the screen.

Ask your unconscious mind to associate the items in the attic with parts of you: your fears; your hopes; your dreams; your beliefs; past problems; current challenges. Some things that you perhaps no longer need to carry around.

Ask your unconscious mind to begin tidying the attic. To re-organise it in any way that works for you. Allow yourself to be drawn to what you need to throw away. What you need to ignore for now, what you want to keep, and have more accessible.

Be relaxed, and accept that you don't need to know why or how – if you simply ask, your unconscious mind will do it for you, quickly, easily, effortlessly. You needed this stuff..... once..... it served a purpose..... but no longer..... you can simply..... let it go. Ask your unconscious mind to organise that which is still useful to you, and you want to keep..... making it easily accessible.

You can, you know, return to the attic many times to re-organise things. And while your unconscious mind continues, all by itself, you can open your eyes, and come back into the room.

The beauty of engaging the unconscious mind in this way is that once you give it the instruction for how you want it to help it can continue doing the work while you get on with other things. It also makes the learning from the past more easily accessible to us, so the past becomes a resource.

Case study: tidying up the unconscious mind

Sadie was a client of mine who had had a difficult childhood. When she cleared out the attic of her unconscious mind using this exercise, she experienced a sense of hope about the future – while she could not undo the past, and while she would have wished things to have been different, what she realised was that she could recognise some of her adult strengths as having their roots in those experiences. She appreciated that her earlier difficulties had given her an unshakeable belief in her ability to cope with whatever life threw at her, and she believed that her earlier experiences had led her to be a good mother to her own children.

Finding your roots again

Many of the challenges we face in adulthood will have their roots in our early years. For some people, their childhood is a place of sadness, for others it is a place of happiness, safety and security. In either case, there are many resources within childhood that would benefit us as adults. Re-connecting with the child you were has a three-fold purpose:

✓ To remind you of how truly loveable you were, and how truly loveable you are.

✓ To offer help and healing to your inner child if he or she needs it.

✓ To appreciate the fun and resilience within children, so you can bring these into your current life stage.

If re-visiting your inner child brings tears, simply allow them to act like a warm cleansing shower to your soul. The important thing to remember is that you are now an adult, and the past, even if painful, is a resource to you. Whatever happened to you, you've survived it, and it's over now.

When you do the following exercise, ensure that you are going to have the opportunity to have some quiet space afterwards - don't do it before you have to rush off to do something else. I suggest you give yourself at least an hour, as you might also want to record your learning in your journal afterwards.

Read the exercise through a couple of times, and trust that your unconscious mind will know what to do. Again, if you want, you can record it and play it back to yourself. If you do this, read it slowly and gently, with lots of pauses.

Exercise: appreciating your inner child

Find a comfortable place, either indoors or out, where you won't be disturbed, and take a few deep slow breaths, until you feel calm and focused. If it helps, you can close your eyes.

Have you ever looked at a newborn baby, and thought how perfect they are? How unblemished, and yet in many ways so apparently wise. We forget that we were once also that baby, and that baby's potential is still in us. As perfect as you were then, that's how perfect you still are inside. And how determined that baby was, to learn to roll over, to sit up, to crawl. Be with that perfect little baby that was you for a moment. You might want to imagine that you are holding it in your arms, telling it how much you love it.

Now think of you as a little toddler. Toddlers are good at saying no, you know. Toddlers really know what they want. Learning to walk, perhaps, and to talk. So many words you learned. Nothing could stop you learning. You were like a sponge, soaking up new experiences. If it feels right to do so, imagine playing with that toddler, as you access the playful, determined parts of yourself. Acknowledge how easily you once learned, and remind yourself that the resource of learning easily is still there, inside you.

Run your thoughts forward a little more, to that young child that was once you, that little boy or girl. Perhaps with some missing front teeth, maybe wearing their school uniform. Skinned knees perhaps. Did that child find learning easy, or were they afraid? Were they starting to feel they might not be good enough, or were they confident in their abilities? In their place in the world? Is there anything you want to say to that child? What relationships did that child have with those around them? Is there any support that they need? You can offer them that now. What would you like to say to them? If anything difficult happened to that young child, remind them they survived. They are grown up now, and safe.

Notice the teenage you, ready to take the world on, perhaps laughing with their friends. Feeling invincible. Feeling you know best, and that life is just out there, waiting. Or perhaps your teenage years were a time of anxiety. Maybe something at home or school worried you. Perhaps you found it hard to fit in. Reassure that teenager that all is well.

In the same way as you can offer that child the protection of the resources and knowledge you have now as an adult, they can remind you that that connection with who you were is still there, still part of who you are. All the resources they had, you still have. Ask that little you if there is anything they need from you. Offer them unconditional love. Think of any fun activities you longed to do as a child. You can do them again, or if they were not available to that younger you, then perhaps you can do them now. If anything bad happened to that younger you, ask if it still hurts. Reassure that child that no matter what happened to them, they survived. That you can take care of them now; that they no longer have to struggle.

Sometimes it helps to imagine that the child-you is sitting in the adult-you lap. Hold, love and reassure that child that all is well. When you feel ready, fold it back inside.

Know that you can travel to meet this younger you at any time, that they are strong, beautiful and wise. And that they are you.

When you feel ready, gently come back to the present open your eyes, and gradually begin to move around in your chair, feeling the connection with whatever is around you.

You may want to quietly write your reflections about this exercise in your journal.

Case study: healing the inner child

Brian was a manager in an engineering firm. He had several people reporting to him, two of whom had a personality clash, and had frequent rows. They didn't expect Brian to mediate, and they usually sorted things out themselves, without it affecting their performance.

Nevertheless, Brian found that the constant arguing and sniping was so upsetting that it was almost making him ill. He dreaded seeing the two of them together in a meeting, and felt he 'should' as their manager be able to sort it out. What he wanted to do though was to put his hands over his ears and shut his eyes. In coaching, I asked him to do exactly that, and see where it took him. Within a few seconds, he was describing himself as a four year old, sitting in his bedroom with his eyes shut and his hands over his ears as his parents argued noisily downstairs. It was emotional for him to access this memory, which was one he realised had occurred frequently throughout his childhood. At the time, he experienced a sense of helplessness, and feeling he 'should' be able to do something to resolve it, but was unclear what.

The adult Brian was then able to reassure the little child that he no longer needed to cope with this situation, and that the adult Brian would deal with it from now on. He told the child that he could relax; it wasn't his responsibility to sort out rows between grown-ups.

The learning Brian took from this was that there was a still a little child part of him inside trying to take responsibility for fixing things, and it popped up every time there was a conflict situation – unfortunately by using the same techniques it had used 35 years previously. Once the child realised it no longer had to do this, Brian felt able to deal with the issue as an adult.

Pass the eraser: re-drawing your pictures

Earlier in the book I talked above about Tracey accessing an old memory of being bullied. In her case, that understanding of where her current difficulties were coming from was enough to help her let them go, but what if your memory keeps popping up in your face? You can deal with that by learning how to store the memory differently.

Case study: haunted by an old memory

Josie came for presentation skills training. When she stood in front of a group, she described an expectation of total humiliation. She felt sick, shaky and panic-stricken, and was convinced that at any moment something awful would happen, and that everyone would laugh at her. Josie was already very aware of a traumatic imprint memory. When she was 7, her class teacher had to take a few days compassionate leave, and cover was provided by a student teacher. This teacher was very unsympathetic to children asking to use the toilet, and told them they had to wait for a break. She also insisted that when doing reading practice, a child had to stand at the front and read aloud to the group. Josie was a shy child, although she was a very able reader. In her anxiety about being in front of the group, she fluffed a few words. The teacher had shouted at her to speak up, and in complete terror, Josie had wet herself in front of the class. From that point, she said that the picture of her humiliation, the sounds of the laughter, and the feelings associated with it popped into her mind every time she had to stand in front of a group.

What's happening here is that Josie is having some difficulty sorting real from imagined, and every time she experienced what she saw as a threat, it triggered the response as if it was still real, and not something that had happened to her 25 years previously.

Over the course of a single coaching session, Josie was able to change that memory so that it no longer had the same emotional hold on her.

First I asked Josie to describe not the content of the picture, but what NLP calls its *sub-modalities*. These are features and qualities of the picture. Josie's picture of that memory was big and bright, right in front of her face, with shrill background noise and she had what she described as a 'football-sized', hard, unyielding feeling in the pit of her stomach. She was also associated into the picture. What I mean by that is that Josie was actually inside herself in the picture - when she looked down, what she could see were her wet shoes and the puddle on the floor. This meant that every time Josie thought about the memory she essentially got back inside that scared and helpless little girl.

I asked her to step out of the picture, so she was looking at herself as if it was a photo or digital image. I then asked her what feeling she would like to have when standing in front of a group, and she decided a soft fluttery one would be best. Josie was then given the instruction to move the picture as far away from her as it would go, until it was a tiny speck in the distance, while making the colours faded and washed out. At the same time, she was to replace the shrill sound with some relaxing music of her choice, and experience a soft fluttery feeling inside.

After she had practised this a few time, it was becoming increasingly hard for her to get all the detail of the old picture back.

I then had her imagine herself standing in front of a group, and notice what was different. Josie said that when she thought about the next time she would have to make a presentation, all she felt was a gentle fluttery feeling inside, and she felt calm and relaxed.

Now it's your turn!

Exercise: re-drawing your memories

This exercise will help you to change how you store your memories so that you experience them differently. It has several steps:

- ✓ Think of a memory that makes you feel a bit anxious, embarrassed or irritated when you think about it, and make a picture. Make sure that you step out of the picture, so that you are looking at it as if it was a photo.

✓ Now push the picture further and further away from you. Perhaps it moves faster the further away it gets. As it moves away, notice how it shrinks down to almost nothing.

✓ At the same time, have all the colour drain right out of it. If you want to, you can shrink it to such a size that it simply disappears right over the horizon.

✓ Now, try to get that memory back, while **keeping it way out of sight**, and notice how the feelings have changed.

It really is that simple to re-draw our old memories. Now a couple of things. Remember that for this to work you don't need to be an expert at visualisation – if you can recall the colour of your front door, then you are visualising.

The other point is that if you can do this with poor memories, you can also do it with happy ones. Think for a minute of a happy memory from your past. As you think about that memory, see what you saw, hear what you heard, feel what you felt. Notice more and more detail.

As you do that, you will probably already be starting to experience feeling happy, or motivated, or energised, or whatever the main feeling associated with that memory was. Now, make it even better – make the picture bigger and brighter, and perhaps step right into it, and experience it again from the inside. And that's how easy to is to make the past a resource!

Pressing the delete key: redrafting the old stories

I want to say a bit about stories now. We all tell ourselves stories all the time. That's great if they are good empowering stories. But what if they are stories that hold us back, embarrass us, make us feel afraid to move on?

We use our old stories as a lens to interpret and make sense of our current reality, which is why it's important to examine them.

The important thing to remember about stories is that they are your representation of reality, not the reality itself. At this point, people I coach sometimes get upset and say 'Are you saying I'm not telling you the truth? I've had some terrible experiences!'

I'm sure they have, and I have a lot of empathy for them, and admiration for how many people overcome a less than perfect start in life. However, as a coach, I have a choice. I can allow them to tell and re-tell their story, with me making sympathetic noises. But you know what? They've probably already done that hundreds of times. Has it helped? Almost certainly not, or they wouldn't be seeing me. What people need is a means of moving on from their stories. Nowhere in my contract is a sympathy clause, and I would suggest that you consider not having one in the contract you make with yourself.

> *There is nothing either good or bad, but thinking makes it so.*
>
> *Hamlet*

I came to coaching and NLP from an interest in counselling. Part of the process involved us having counselling ourselves. I found lots of stories to tell, and over time I noticed that rather than feeling better, I was becoming more and more focused on some of the sad and difficult things that had happened to me. In the process of paraphrasing what I said and reflecting it back to me it was as if the counsellor re-imprinted the stories. So if she said something like 'you sounded very sad when you said that', even if I hadn't been, I went inside, made a picture of what being sad was like, got the feeling of sadness, and before I knew it, I had added a new feeling to my story.

For some people and in some contexts counselling may be helpful, especially when dealing with unresolved issues of loss and bereavement, but for many that re-telling of old stories just embeds them more firmly.

Just as you can't look at a map and say it is the same as the territory it represents, you can't tell a story and say it is what actually happened. The process is that something happens; and because you can't pay attention to every single aspect of the experience, you will delete, distort and generalise details. Some of these may be insignificant, others may be important. You will create an internal image, often with sounds and feelings, of what happened. So the story is distorted once. When you re-tell the story, you again delete, distort and generalise more stuff you don't believe is important. Then the person you are telling it to will do the same, and go through the entire delete, distort and generalise process yet again. This is why witness statements are notoriously unreliable. I have a friend who is a police officer. He was recently called to a break-in at a convenience store. Witness statements placed the perpetrator as black, white or Asian. He was between 5 foot 4 inches and 6 feet tall; 20 to 40 years old; and was wearing a baseball jacket, a football shirt, or motor cycle leathers. He was carrying a gun, a knife or no weapon at all. About the only feature that everyone agreed on was that it had been a man. Everyone believed they were telling the truth, but each witness had deleted, distorted and generalised the incident, based on their own beliefs, attitudes, social influences and memories. They created a representation of what had happened.

If you tell yourself a story in which you believe you are brave, powerful and smart, then that is useful, and you will filter for things that back up that story – and you will find them. Conversely if you tell yourself a story that presents you as weak, powerless or lacking in intelligence, then you will filter for evidence to back that story up – and you will find it.

Stories often have their roots in family lore: 'She's the clever one', 'He's the athlete', and 'She was always an airhead'; or in messages you received in school: 'You'll never amount to anything', 'You're not one of the brighter kids'.

So how do you deal with these stories? The first thing is to become aware of them. If there is a lot of negative emotion attached, especially anger, sadness, fear or guilt, then it is usually better to deal with them with the support of an experienced NLP therapist and coach. They may well teach you NLP techniques called *Time-code interventions* to assist you to unhook the difficult emotion from the story, so you can let it go. It won't wipe your memory banks clean - that's not the purpose of these techniques - but once the emotion is removed, you can look at them dispassionately, without distress, take any learning you need from them (remember, the past is a resource) and then move on.

Case study: the story-teller

Karen ran lots of stories – while some of them were entertaining, they all ultimately presented her as feckless and incapable. And yet she was anything but – a single mother of a 15 year old, she worked full time, owned a house, and had a full social life. But Karen ran a loop that said (often aloud) 'I'm just pathetic. Got that wrong again. Don't mind me, I'm useless at stuff like this'.

Karen revealed in coaching that she had always felt inferior to her older brother, and when she got pregnant at 17 and decided to keep the baby, her parents had provided lots of evidence of how hopeless she was. The examples ranged from getting pregnant in the first place, to leaving a precious doll out in the rain to be ruined when she was five. The inference being that if she was incapable of looking after a doll, she would be completely irresponsible in charge of a baby.

Karen's coaching homework had a dual purpose – first, she had to interrupt the pattern of negativity, and secondly, having done that, she was to provide evidence to prove the opposite of whatever derogatory remark she had made about herself. She bravely told her friends and colleagues that she wanted their support, so that every time she said something negative about herself, they chanted 'Karen is telling a story!'

While Karen decided to 'out' her problem with her friends and ask for their support, other clients have chosen to take the less exposed route of pinging an elastic band on their wrist. It doesn't actually matter what you do – the aim is to interrupt the story. The next step is to immediately come up with evidence as to why it isn't true. Karen was also asked to keep a list of good attributes she had in her journal. Within two weeks, she had seven pages listing lots of evidence of being strong, powerful and capable – a sort of personal brag list.

Exercise: sorting out your stories

This exercise will help you to get into the habit of picking up the negative stories you tell about yourself, and more importantly, to yourself. You can use Table 2 on page 73 – use a few key words for each story you tell. Next, plan how you are going to interrupt them in future. Here are some ideas for doing this:

- ✓ Pinging an elastic band on your wrist

- ✓ Imagining a big red stop sign or traffic light appearing in front of you

- ✓ Hearing yourself say 'stop' or 'wipe that story' loudly inside

And then IMMEDIATELY bring up an image, memory or feeling of you acting in a different way. If you think you won't be able to find an example quickly, take some time right now to develop a list in the second column of the table, and then use one of these examples every time you need to.

Finally, write down all the evidence you find of yourself acting in a more empowered way. This will help you embed these new stories quickly and effectively.

Table 2: re-drafting the stories

	Stories I tell myself	Alternative stories	Evidence
1.			
2.			
3.			
4.			
5.			
6.			
7.			
8.			
9.			
10.			

The mind body connection

In his fabulous book *Quantum Healing*, Deepak Chopra tells us that every cell in our body is eavesdropping on our internal dialogue. In effect, this means that everything we say to ourselves has an effect on our physiology. Don't just believe me: try this experiment. Sit quietly, and really concentrate on the next paragraph, giving yourself time to concentrate on the words, and the images, feelings, smells and tastes that they evoke.

Exercise: the mind body connection

I would like you to think of a lemon. And as you think of a lemon, make a really clear picture of it. Notice how yellow a lemon is, how shiny the skin is. Look closely at the little dimples in the skin. Now reach out and touch it. Notice that the skin is slightly rough, and perhaps quite cool to the touch. Lift it up, and notice its weight. The heavier lemons are, the juicier they tend to be. You might want to lift it to your nose, so you can smell the faint tanginess of the skin. Imagine digging your thumb nail into the skin, and seeing the fine arc of tart lemon juice, and notice the scent of the juice. Perhaps you can imagine now the lemon on a board in your kitchen. Get a knife, and slice it right down the middle. Look at the flesh, and perhaps run your finger over the wet slippiness, smelling the lemon scent in the air, and noticing the juice trickling on the board. Now lift a piece to your mouth, and just run your tongue over the cut flesh. Mmm, tart, lemony, juice on your tongue.

So, what happened? For lots of people, they notice increased salivation, sometimes a drawing in of their cheeks with the tartness, some even notice a slight ache in their salivary glands. But you know what – there was no lemon! It was only a story.

If simply telling yourself a story for 30 seconds means you produce a bodily response, then think of all the stories you've been telling yourself for the last 20, 30 or 40 years. What sort of influence might they be having? It suddenly becomes clear why the stories had better be good ones, if our bodies are listening so carefully!

So my invitation to you is to work at identifying the stories you are running about yourself, decide which ones are useful, and which ones you will let go, using the exercise on page 72. If you haven't already done so, do it now.

You can be invincible (again): letting go of limiting beliefs

Once upon a time, you believed you could do anything. Think of a baby making the transition from crawling to standing. Does the baby have any doubt it will make it? Does it give up and say that it's too hard, they'll never be able to do it?

But at some point in your life you probably began to make decisions about your own limitations, and these decisions precede the formation of limiting beliefs. Sometimes the belief is formed after one exposure, but more commonly they build up over time. So there we are, six years old and believing we are pretty invincible. And then one day when we are doing our sums, we realise that we've got a lot of them wrong. We aren't too upset, because mum and dad tell us we are pretty special anyway. But then a week later the same thing happens again. We look at the person sitting next to us in class, and notice they have a gold star. We've never had one of those. Maybe next week.

But then next week the teacher speaks to mum, and tells her that we seem to be struggling with our maths. Mum says that she was never any good with numbers either. Suddenly we think about all the things that have happened. We didn't get smiley faces, we didn't get a gold star, and we had to stay in during playtime. Now we form a belief that we aren't good at maths. And since grown-up and invincible mum isn't any good at them either, that probably means we never will be.

Although this is a simple example, we make more serious limiting decisions based about our worth, our skills, and our rights, which will influence every decision we make in the future.

The most important concept I want you to grasp is that we aren't stuck with our beliefs for life. Beliefs can be changed. Think of all the firmly held beliefs you once had that you let go as they no longer served you. Did you once believe in Father Christmas? Do you still believe in him? If you do, then great, but most adults don't.

A personal example: seeing ghosts!

I remember years ago, my parents finally allowed me to stay at home by myself one evening, and while they were out I stayed up late, watched the late night movie, and then went to bed. And then I heard a noise. There was someone on the stairs. And they were getting nearer! I totally believed someone had got into the house, even though I knew my parents had checked the doors and windows before they left, and everything was locked. I jumped out of bed, pulled the dressing table in front of the bedroom door, and sat cowering behind it for what felt like hours till my parents came home. All the time I sat there, I could hear the person breathing on the other side of the door. However the instant my parents opened the front door, and switched on the stair lights, the breathing stopped. As I emerged from the bedroom feeling a bit daft, I realised that what I had heard was the sound of the house cooling down. Within the space of about 15 minutes, I had managed to install a real and very scary belief that there was someone in the house. And as soon as mum and dad were safely home, I let that belief go again.

Do you know how elephants are trained in captivity? Apparently the trick is to teach the elephant it's 'place' in the world while it is still very young, by ensuring it develops a very limiting and erroneous belief about its own strength. To do this, a heavy metal chain is attached to its rear leg, so it can't move away. Initially the baby will struggle and fight the limitation, but gradually it realises that it's useless to struggle, and all that happens is that they cause themselves pain. Gradually they come to accept that they can only travel the distance of the chain, and eventually they lose heart, and give up the struggle. After some time, they no longer even tug at the chain, and they stay well inside the perimeter of movement allowed them by the chain.

As the elephant gets older, the weight of the chain is gradually reduced – it is often possible simply to tie a light cord round the leg, without even attaching it to anything, and the elephant will not wander away. Even though the adult elephant would be more than capable of breaking loose, it doesn't even try. It has now been fully conditioned to accept its limitations. In other words, the elephant has a limiting belief about how the world works.

Do you want to be like the elephant, stuck with a belief that effectively keeps you tethered, totally believing in your own weakness? Perhaps you can already recognise times in your adult life when you've been held fast by a childhood belief? You probably learned the lesson of staying in your place, whatever that was, as well as the elephant does. That doesn't mean that you had to have experienced abuse or trauma – perhaps it was just a drip-feed to not doing as well as people hoped you might, of not being suited to the learning environment you found yourself in, or of feeling that somehow you were a disappointment. Perhaps you were led to believe that you couldn't handle things, that the world was a dangerous place, or that someone else happiness depending on you behaving in certain ways.

Do you want to move on? Then first of all, get some really good, empowering beliefs in your filters. Is it really that easy? Yes, absolutely. Let's look at some ways of doing this.

Exercise: do you really believe that?

This exercise has several steps. You don't have to do it all at once, and sometimes it helps to let your unconscious mind mull over the answers to each step before you move on.

- ✓ In your journal, make two lists. List one is all the limiting beliefs you currently have about yourself. List two is all the great, empowering beliefs that you have. Most people find it relatively easy to come up with the first four or five items on each list, as these are usually fairly consciously held. Keep asking yourself the question 'and what else?', until you have at least 10 items on each list.

- ✓ Look at them carefully, and identify the three beliefs in each list that have the most impact on your life. Three great beliefs that you absolutely would not want to let go of, and three limiting beliefs that are seriously holding you back.

✓ Identify how you can maximise the impact of the great beliefs. For example, if you have a belief that you are a good friend, how could you use the personal qualities which support that belief in different contexts?

✓ Now look at your limiting beliefs – the three 'biggies' that are seriously holding you back. I'm going to ask you to do something tough now. I want now to completely associate into the experience of living your life while carrying these beliefs around with you. One of my clients said it helped to imagine them as huge boulders he was never allowed to put down, and had to be juggled with in every interaction he made from now on. If that imagery works for you, then use it – if not, find your own. The main point is that you experience how truly limited your life is while you have these beliefs. Not only now, but in the future, as they become heavier and more entrenched.

✓ Are you ready to change? Take each of those three limiting beliefs, and write down what you would like to believe instead. Make these beliefs positive. For example, if you have a limiting belief that you are stupid, the great belief is **not** 'I'm not stupid', it's something like 'I can learn quickly and easily whenever I want to'.

✓ Now challenge yourself to find evidence of the limiting beliefs **not** being true. This is the process of loosening off the old belief. At the same time, you are starting to build a scaffold that will take you towards some new beliefs.

✓ From now on, focus on these new beliefs. Some clients find it helpful to say them to themselves in the mirror, others leave notes around the house reminding them of the new belief – find creative ways that work for you. As you start to integrate these new beliefs, you will start to filter the world differently, and you will notice more and more evidence for them which will strengthen your scaffold.

Figure 2: challenging old beliefs

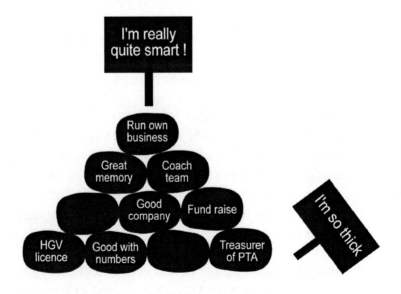

The whole is more than the sum of the parts: becoming whole again

For many clients, when I talk about letting go limiting beliefs and creating new ones, I notice a sense of internal conflict. A 'yes but' feeling. Although people may be willing to identify a new belief, if you don't also let go of the old one, then the new belief might be held mainly at the conscious level, and your old or conflicting belief is held unconsciously. So every time you state the new belief, the old one pops up from your unconscious mind in an attempt to override it. Although it is possible to overcome this by acting 'as if' the more helpful belief is true until you imprint it in your nervous system, there is a way of integrating new beliefs quickly, easily and painlessly. In the process of integrating the new belief, you dump the old one – a sort of two for one offer.

I used this very effectively with Gillian, a 14 year old who was brought to me by her mum for hypnosis for exam nerves. I taught Gillian relaxation techniques and self hypnosis, and while they undoubtedly helped her, Gillian still experienced a sense of 'yes, but' when she thought about doing her exams. Gillian really wanted to believe that she could do exams easily, but she felt that something was blocking her. When I spoke to Gillian at length about what she believed about herself there was clearly a conflict. On the one hand, she believed that she was capable of passing her exams, but on the other, she had a belief that deep down she was stupid, and under pressure she would fail.

Case study: integrating conflicting parts

I asked Gillian to get the part that believed she was stupid out on her hand, and to give it a little body and personality. She described it as anxious, like Mrs Tiggywinkle in the Beatrix

Potter books, fussing about, and wearing an apron. When prompted, she said the voice was her grandmother. I used an NLP technique called *chunking* to find out the highest intention of that Mrs Tiggywinkle part – which was, ultimately, to keep Gillian safe from feeling let down and disappointed in herself. Gillian looked surprised when she said that, as clearly she had been viewing that part as something she had to fight against – but usually parts that are limiting us do have a positive intention, they just aren't necessarily expressed in a useful way.

We then turned to the part that believed she was capable. Gillian personified this part as a Luke Skywalker type character from Star Wars, brave and fearless. Again, we chunked up to the highest intention of the part, and Gillian was amazed to discover that it too wanted her to be safe and to avoid feeling let down and disappointed. As I pointed out to Gillian that the parts shared a positive intention, I suggested that she brought her hands together, and have the parts merge, sharing all the positivity. As she did this, the anxiety visibly dropped from her face, and her shoulders relaxed. I gently suggested that she might want to bring this new part inside, and feel the positivity and confidence that comes from having all your parts fully integrated and aligned.

Now this isn't magic - Gillian still had to work hard to pass her exams, but she said that from that point, she no longer had that nagging feeling of not being good enough.

An indication that you may have conflicting beliefs or parts that would benefit from being integrated is if you find yourself saying things like 'I really want to believe this, but.....' or 'a part of me knows I can, but a part just seems to be holding me back'. If you notice this happening, then do the following exercise. Read through it first to familiarise yourself with the steps.

Exercise: becoming aligned

Find yourself a quiet spot where you won't be disturbed for half an hour. Sit quietly, and take two or three slow deep breaths in and out.

Identify the parts holding the two conflicting beliefs.

Imagine that the negative one is sitting on one of your hands – if it were to have a shape and a personality, notice what it would be.

On the other hand, put the part that has the other belief. Again, notice what shape and personality it has.

Now you are going to talk to the negative belief first. Ask it, 'What is it that you are trying to do for me?' Wait until you feel an answering response coming – some people find it helps to talk out loud, and to answer as if they were the part. Initially, what you hear may seem quite negative, but keep asking 'for what purpose do you want that?' Eventually you will begin to get answers that start to reveal the true positive intent of that part that is holding the old belief. Once you get that, turn and imagine that you are looking at the part with the conflicting belief in your other hand.

Go through the same process with this. You may well find that this part is more transparent, and that you get to the positive intent quickly. You will probably also find that the positive intentions of each part are very similar.

When you are satisfied that you understand the positive intent of each part, have your hands come gently together, and experience the sense of the parts merging into one. Notice the sensation for a moment.

Thank the parts for having your highest purpose in mind, and imagine that you are bringing them back into yourself. Some people like to imagine them floating in, others like to wrap their arms around themselves and give themselves a hug, others like to clasp their hands to their chest. Whatever feels right for you is the right thing to do.

Sit quietly for 10 minutes, and experience a sense of stillness and calm, knowing that the internal conflict is over now, and that your conscious and your unconscious mind are working together in harmony.

After you've done this exercise, it is often helpful to record what you notice in your journal. You can do this technique more than once – generally, the more conflicts you can resolve and integrate, the more quickly you can move forward.

Time travel anyone? Over-writing limiting beliefs

This technique is a time-code intervention. It's an extremely useful technique, and is based on original work on *Time Line Therapy*™ by Tad James and Wyatt Woodsmall; and on *Memory Resolution* by Dr Susi Strang and Craig Wood.

It works from the premise that not only do we have past memories, but that we also have future memories, which simply haven't been created or realised yet. Furthermore, each of us will store our memories systematically, in a way that is unique to us. When we think of these memories, we might access them as pictures, sounds or feelings, and they will be located in some way in relation to our physical body.

Before you do this process it's important that you remind yourself about the process of association and dissociation. Dissociation means that you are looking at a situation from the outside, as if you are watching a movie of yourself. There is little if any emotion. Association means that you are actually inside the situation, and experiencing it, with all the emotion that is attached to the situation.

Let's practice this. Think of the experience of brushing your teeth. Now imagine standing at your bathroom door, and watching yourself doing this. Depending on where the door is in relation to the sink, you may be looking at your back. You may see your head bent over the sink. You may see one arm bent up towards your head, and it may be moving back and forward or up and down. You may notice the other arm either by your side, or resting on the edge of the sink. This is a **dissociated** position.

Now make another picture of you cleaning your teeth. In this picture, you can feel the toothbrush in your hand. You can experience the sensation of the toothbrush in your mouth. You can taste the toothpaste. When you look down, you can see your arm, but you can't see your face or head without looking in a mirror. This is an **associated** position. The following exercise is done entirely from a **dissociated** position.

Exercise: putting new beliefs in your memory storage system

The exercise is in two parts.

First of all, you are going to explore how you store your past and future memories. Let's think about teeth cleaning again for a minute.

- ✓ Think about cleaning your teeth this morning. Notice where that memory is located in relation to you. Everyone is unique – there are no right answers.

- ✓ Now think about cleaning your teeth a week ago, and notice where you place that memory in relation to you.

- ✓ Now think about cleaning your teeth six or nine months ago – perhaps when you were on holiday. Notice where that memory is in relation to you.

- ✓ And finally, think of cleaning your teeth in your future, and notice where the location of that future memory is.

- ✓ Join the location of all the memories!. That is your memory storage system.

- ✓ Before we move to the second part of the exercise, practice detaching or separating yourself from this storage system. Perhaps you could float above it, so you have a bird's eye view of the entire system. Or perhaps you could be in a helicopter, flying above it. Whatever works for you.

Now that you understand your own unique method of storing memories, you can use it as a means of letting go of limiting beliefs, and of negative emotions. Here we are going to concentrate on letting go of limiting beliefs. This works well as a self-help measure. However, if you have significant trauma or abuse attached to the belief, or there is a major phobia involved, then you should seek professional support. At the back of this book you will find details of organisations that can put you in touch with suitably qualified practitioners.

Let's move on to the second part.

- ✓ Think of a belief you have that you wish you didn't.

- ✓ Float up above your memory storage system, so that you have a high bird's eye view.

- ✓ Float all the way back your memory storage system till you find the point at which you developed that limiting belief.

- ✓ Ask yourself what you can learn from that event.

- ✓ Go back to just before the event actually happened, and transmit additional resources both to yourself, and anyone else involved in the incident, which would have enabled you to develop a different and more empowering belief.

- ✓ And then in your own time, float all the way back to the present, noticing how everything is different as you live your life with a different belief, and with the new learning.

✓ Feel confident about going forward into the future.

Remember to record your findings in your journal!

Releasing old emotions can be emotional! However, this process should not be traumatic. Many clients experience a sense of relief and optimism after completing this exercise. The key is to ensure that you float well above your memory storage system – you do NOT need to relive the experience. You are simply a curious observer.

Case study: helping himself to self-belief

Eli is a young man who had under-achieved for most of his life. He had dropped out of university after failing his second year exams, and had several failed relationships. He was now with a new partner who said she was fed up living on tenterhooks waiting for him to press what she described as his self-destruct button. He was sceptical about this process, but when he did this exercise, he floated back in time till he was watching an incident that had happened when he was 6 years old. He had come in from playtime to collect his biscuit from his schoolbag, and heard his current and previous teachers discussing him. They were saying that no one in his family ever amounted to much, and while he seemed to be better than his older siblings, they had no doubt that he would turn out just like them.

The adult Eli decided to transmit resources such as self-belief and resilience to the younger Eli. At the same time, he transmitted resources such as tolerance and open-mindedness to his teachers. He felt that if all those resources had been in place at the time, he would have lived a different life and had a belief that he could overcome his home-life challenges and fully utilise the fact that he was extremely bright.

He then floated back to the present, noticing how things would have been different with this new belief.

After the session, Eli and I had a conversation about the need to remain at cause with this new information. It wouldn't have been helpful for him to shift his self-hatred onto his teachers, and blame them for everything that had happened to him. A useful concept here is that everyone is doing the best they can with the resources that they have. His teachers were doing the best they could – they were young, relatively inexperienced and working in a tough school. Eli had also done the best he could do at the time. His new beliefs though had given him new resources, and from now on he could make different choices. The outcome of this story is that Eli went back to university and eventually became a teacher himself. He married that woman who had insisted he sorted himself out, and they have two children of their own now. Eli is convinced that accessing his memory storage system and sending that little boy who was him some additional resources was the turning point in his life.

Cutting the cords

This is primarily an exercise about forgiveness. Forgiveness is a difficult concept sometimes, especially if we have been done great wrong. I would never say that anyone 'should' forgive anyone else (except possibly yourself), as I am not in a position to judge what has been done to you. I also don't believe that to say you forgive someone means that you say that it was alright for them to have done what they did – all you are doing is severing the emotional attachment that comes with not forgiving.

I do believe that when we hold onto rage and anger, then there is a cost to us as well. We use energy that we could be directing elsewhere, and it maintains a connection with that person that would not be there if we forgave and cut the cord. So if there are people in your past who have hurt you in some way, then this exercise can be helpful. At the end of the day though, it comes down to you making the decision to simply let the past go. In doing so, you start a process of self-healing.

> *He that cannot forgive breaks the bridge over which he himself must cross; for every man has need of forgiveness.*
>
> Thomas Fuller

You will need to allow at least 30 minutes for this exercise, as you might want some quiet reflective space afterwards. Read through the directions a few times, and then once you have the basic outline, trust that your unconscious mind will know what to do.

Exercise: cutting the cords that bind you

First, find a quiet spot, indoors or out, where you won't be disturbed.

Make yourself comfortable, and allow yourself to become relaxed. Take a few deep slow breaths in and out, and check your body for any tension. Breathe relaxation into that spot. Ensure that your shoulders are relaxed, your jaw is loose, and your hands are resting lightly in your lap. If it helps, close your eyes.

Allow the image of a stage to appear in front of you. On that stage, let an image appear of someone with whom you have unresolved issues. Imagine a thin cord binding you together.

Look at them carefully. Ask yourself 'What did I need to learn from you?' Acknowledge the ties that bind you. Imagine yourself saying to them 'I forgive you, go now'. As you allow this image to fade, imagine that you have cut or severed the cord. You no longer have a connection with this person. You have learned what you needed to learn, and they are gone now.

Take a few calming and cleansing breaths. Feel at peace.

You can repeat this part of the exercise as often as you need to.

When you are ready, open your eyes, and come back to full awareness.

Record your experiences in your journal.

Do you see sunshine or showers?

We have options about how we view the past: while we can't change what happened to us, we can certainly change how we choose to deal with it. That doesn't mean that we shouldn't acknowledge times of grief, hurt or loss, or indeed that we shouldn't feel these emotions – sometimes they are the absolutely appropriate emotions to feel.

> *There are always flowers for those who want to see them.*
>
> *Henri Matisse*

I'd like to end this section by telling you a story. It's on some levels a child's story, and one we can learn from. I've heard it many times over the years, and perhaps you have too. It was most recently told to me by the seven year old daughter of a friend of mine.

Annie and I were having a story telling session, and after about an hour, my creativity was running dry, as she prefers 'made-up' stories, to stories out of books. Eventually she said to me 'I have a story – I'll tell it to you. It's one you'll like'.

So we cuddled up together, and this is how the story goes:

Once upon a time, deep in the woods, lived a little tiny deer. The deer had never been to the edge of the woods, so she had never seen the sky. She lived deep, deep in the forest, where all was still and quiet, and the deer lived happily. She nibbled the trees, and the grass, and when it rained, water dripped through the trees for the deer to drink. She believed she had everything she needed.

However, one day, the deer wandered right to the very edge of the forest, and she was amazed at what she saw. For the very first time in her life, she saw the sky, and the sun. The fresh new grass tickled her toes, and the deer was full of wonder as she danced along on the soft grass. She spoke to the cows and the sheep, and generally had a wonderful time.

And then she came to a little pond. She didn't know what it was, and she was so excited, until she looked into the pond and saw: a little deer, stuck in the water! She reached a hoof into the water, but although the other deer reached a hoof back out to her, she couldn't see any way to pull her out.

In terror, the little deer raced back to the edge of the wood, and begged her friend the badger to help. Mr Badger was very cross at being disturbed during the day, but he went back with the little deer. When he looked in the pond, he too jumped back with amazement. 'That's not a deer', he said 'that's a badger! What is IT doing out during the day? We are going to have to rescue it'.

So the deer and the badger rushed back in a panic, and got their friend the mole to come. She didn't like being out in such bright sunshine, but her two friends were in such a state that she went with them. She looked into the pond, and she said 'That's not a deer ..... or a badger..... that's a mole! How on earth are we going to rescue it?'

The three friends stood discussing the problem at the edge of the pool. They were all very upset by this time, and all were wishing they hadn't taken the risk of leaving the forest. Clearly when they looked at the evidence of their eyes, the outside world was a dangerous place. Meanwhile, the wise old owl was circling overhead, watching what was going on. Eventually, he sighed, and decided to help out the three friends.

The wise old owl picked up a twig, and flew overhead, and dropped the twig in the water. And as the three friends watched, the ripples spread across the pond. The owl asked, 'What can you see now?' The friends looked in the water, and realised that the pool was completely empty. The deer, and the badger and the mole had completely disappeared. There was no one at all stuck in the pond.

The owl asked the three friends 'What have you learned?' The friends looked at one another. 'Well', said the wise old owl, 'You have learned that sometimes you can actually talk yourself into having a problem when none exists – you've just been looking at it the wrong way'.

'Now', said Annie, 'Wasn't that a GOOD story?'

Out of the mouths of babes – and perhaps you would like to reflect on the fact that sometimes you just need to look at your problems in a different way.

CHECKPOINT

This section of the book has focused on helping you develop the skills and techniques which will allow you to coach yourself to release negative stuff from your past, clearing the way for you to use the past as a resource. Already you have a range of skills in your self-coaching toolbox. You should now understand:

✓ The role of your unconscious mind

✓ Visualisation as a means of clearing the past

✓ How to nurture your inner child

✓ How to change your internal pictures using sub-modalities

✓ How to re-write your life stories

✓ How to integrate conflicting parts

✓ How to let go of limiting beliefs

✓ How to cut the cords

You should be recording your progress in your journal, taking a daily temperature reading, and reflecting on your experiences of the exercises, so that you can get them 'in the muscle'. Remember that success is built up by stacking lots of good habits, one on top of the other. The converse of this is that failure is created simply by letting a lot of poor habits stack up on each other. Which are you going to choose?

Already, you know more about taking control of your life and re-programming your mind, so give yourself a huge message of appreciation for getting this far.

Remember that the unconscious mind is vast, and even if you have worked through all the exercises in this section, at some point in the future, something may pop up from your unconscious mind. The difference now though is that you have the knowledge and skills to deal with it.

Next, let's move on look at what is going on in your life at the moment, and explore how you can think and act differently in order to create a brighter future.

4

THE HERE AND NOW

ROUTE PLANNER

Have you ever heard the saying 'Yesterday *is history, tomorrow is a mystery, today is a gift, which is why it's called the present?* 'Do you ever find yourself going over and over the past, or worrying endlessly about the future? Perhaps to the extent that you find little joy in the present moment?

This section focuses on being real and authentic right now. Do you ever wonder why it is that some people appear to have all the luck in life? By the end of this section you will be able to change how you view the world so that you can get the same. You will have assessed your current levels of satisfaction with different areas of your life. You will be clearer about your values and life purpose, and have tools for helping you to prioritise and build better relationships. You will be able to use visualisation as a self healing tool, and you will be clear about what really matters to you.

EXERCISES IN THIS SECTION

Making a success board	60 minutes
Compulsion versus choice	10 minutes
Wheel of Life	20 minutes
How satisfied are you?	60 minutes
What is success?	30 minutes
Your values hierarchy	20 minutes
Your life purpose	30 minutes
Moving to solution focused thinking	30 minutes
It's good to talk	30 minutes
Defining your priorities	30 minutes
Healing meditation	30 minutes
Two minute meditation	2 minutes
What is your end goal?	30 minutes

GETTING POSITIVE

The temptation with coaching is to get straight into goal setting mode, but we've got lots of work to do before we reach that point. After all, you are going to be living with the outcomes of your goals for a long time, so it's worth doing some groundwork to get them right.

> *Forever is composed of nows.*
>
> Emily Dickinson

Before we do anything else though, I want you to get in touch with the inner cheerleader we talked about in Step 2. Sit down with him/her. Have a cup of tea, a glass of wine, whatever. You are about to have a conversation with your new best pal.

Ask them:

- ✓ What do I do really well?

- ✓ What should I be really proud of?

And no censoring the answers. This is big appreciation time, so get lots of good stuff out in your journal. And if that old voice shows up, then just gag it! And now have them ask you the questions:

- ✓ What brings you joy at the moment?

- ✓ What do you want to do differently?

- ✓ What just feels right?

Remember to check in with your inner cheerleader frequently. Earlier in this book we talked about the need for support to help you change and achieve your goals. Your cheerleader is a vital part of that, and they are always there.

GET INTO SUCCESS MODE

What does success mean to you? It tends to mean different things to different people. When I first started working in this field, I remember being put off by motivational speakers whose measure of success seemed to be how big their house was, how many energy-guzzling cars they owned, and how big their boat was. These just weren't the kind of things that excited me. Furthermore, if these material things are the ones that you use to measure your success, and you haven't yet achieved them to your satisfaction, it's very easy to get into 'I'm a failure' mode. Much more useful is to get yourself into a positive frame of mind about what you have achieved in life so far, so that your focus remains on your resourcefulness and creativity.

Exercise: making a success board

This focus will help you create the success you want in your future. While you can simply generate a list in your journal if that works best for you, many of my clients find it more useful to use this as an opportunity to re-connect with some of the creativity of childhood, and do it as a bright and colourful collage.

For this you will need a big sheet of paper – flip chart paper is fine, or you can cut a piece off a roll of wallpaper. Gather some brightly coloured felt pens, pictures from magazines and some glue, and start to create a visual reminder of everything you have achieved in life so far. Go as far back as you can, and remember that no achievement is too small to be recorded. So winning the three-legged race at school goes in there, along with learning to ride your bike, getting your first pay cheque, your first promotion. Everything! Pin it up where you can see it, and every time something else pops into your mind, get it up on your collage. And if the old voice shows up saying 'Well, that was nothing, everyone got a prize that year' just invite it to go, in whatever way works for you! What you are doing with this exercise is developing reference experiences for being successful. The adult-you maybe thinks getting the stabilisers off your bike was no big deal, but if you go back into that little child you were, I bet you felt pretty good about yourself at the time. It's that feeling of pride and possibility that will be a resource to you in the future.

After you have done this exercise, think about other people in your life who you see as 'successful'. How do you think they got where they are, and have the success they have? Many people will say that it's down to luck, or to circumstances of birth, or fate. It's a tempting get-out clause, but I have a different view of it. Gary Player, the golfer, said that the harder he worked, the luckier he got. Essentially this means that luck is the result of effort, and effort is the result of choices. Think about what you might achieve if you were willing to make choices, again and again, that moved you towards what you wanted. Success is about consistently doing things that move you towards your goal. All that may be stopping you is some beliefs you have about yourself, or about the way the world works – and those beliefs are nothing but thoughts or stories you've told yourself again and again until they seem true. I'm going to be challenging you to come up with some different thoughts! The real truth is that you are capable of so much more. Marianne Williamson, in *A Course in Miracles,* writes: 'Our deepest fear is not that we are inadequate. Our deepest fear is that we are powerful beyond measure. It is our light, not our darkness that most frightens us. We ask ourselves, 'Who am I to be brilliant, gorgeous, talented, and fabulous?' Actually, who are you *not* to be? Your playing small does not serve the world. There is nothing enlightened about shrinking so that other people won't feel insecure around you.'

Let's start to look at how you can achieve that experience of being totally committed to your own success, and to letting your light shine.

WHAT COLOUR ARE YOUR FILTERS?

In previous sections I've mentioned that we have a set of filters or lenses, through which we view the world. One of the most effective ways to begin to have more success in your life - whatever that means to you - is to begin to explore what you are holding in your filters, give them a good clean out, and put more useful stuff in there.

Figure 3: how we filter the world

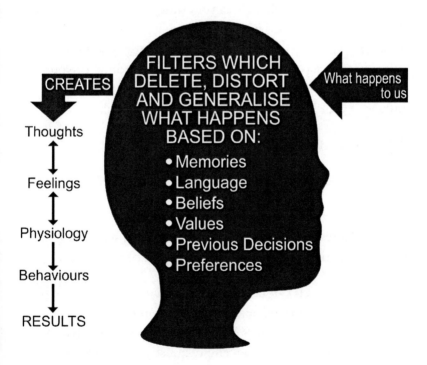

In essence, what happens is that we have a mass of information bombarding us every minute of the day. This comes into our brain through our senses of sight, hearing, touch, taste and smell.

We run that information through a set of filters, which we use to delete, distort, and generalise the information that has come in. These filters are made up of everything that has happened to us from the day we were born. They hold the messages we got from our parents, or teachers, our friends. They hold the stories we have told ourselves, and the conversations we've had with other people. Basically, there is a LOT of stuff in there, and everything new that happens to us is passed through these filters so we can make sense of it. What is left after the filtering process is then used to create what NLP calls an *internal representation* – you could perhaps loosely describe this as your thoughts about something. That thought combines with your physiology: how you are breathing, standing etc, and that in turn creates what in NLP is called a *state* – again, loosely described as an emotion or your feelings about something. Those things in combination will influence your behaviour, and ultimately your results.

The filtering processes

The filtering process itself is essential, and does three things:

- ✓ *Deletion* is the process of ignoring things that are of no interest to us. We'd go mad otherwise if we had to pay attention to absolutely everything all of the time.

- ✓ *Distortion* is our creativity. An architect can look at a piece of waste ground, and through the process of distortion, can envisage homes built there. Distortion is what enables us to view an empty house, and be planning where our Christmas tree will sit; or to look at a sample of wallpaper, and decide whether it will suit our room or not.

✓ *Generalisation* gives us the ability to draw conclusions from minimal information. For example, when we think of a chair, we might all be thinking about something that looks quite different, but what we will all have in common is a piece of furniture that you can sit on.

So far so good! However, these processes can also hinder us. Because of the stories we have told ourselves over the years, and the beliefs we have about the world, we might choose to delete opportunities. We just don't notice things. Some people are described as lucky, but often when you question them it turns out that they simply were open to possibility, and noticed opportunities. Sometimes we distort situations in ways that upset or frighten us, or we make generalisations about things in disabling ways. For example, perhaps a teacher once looked at me in a certain way, and then gave me a punishment exercise. I might then make a generalisation that everyone in the future who looked at me in the same way was going to punish me, so I would develop a set of avoidance strategies. They might have served me well, once upon a time, with that teacher, but they are unlikely to be good strategies in the workplace.

> **All battles are first won or lost in the mind.**
>
> Joan of Arc

So cleaning up your filters matters! Sports people for example, will spend a lot of time working on what is called the *inner-game.* They understand that they need to hold only good things in their filters, in order for them to perform at their best. Even if they fail at something, you will often hear them afterwards completely re-framing it as a learning experience, so that it becomes positive.

You can also develop an inner game for life, to ensure that you begin to filter for what you want.

So what is it that actually does the filtering?

Everybody's filters are unique to them (remember the example of the burglary at the convenience store?), but they are based around the same few things:

- ✓ Beliefs

- ✓ Values

- ✓ Preferences

- ✓ Decisions

- ✓ Language and self-talk

Let's look at each of these in turn in a bit more detail.

Beliefs

Our beliefs are our off/on switches about what we can and can't do. A simple belief about something, for example 'I could never learn to swim', immediately shuts off all possibility of learning. A more empowering belief might be 'I can learn to swim if I choose to do so'. It doesn't deny the reality that you can't currently swim (it wouldn't be safe or appropriate to have that belief if it isn't true), but it does open up the possibility that you can learn. It also emphasises choice, so it puts you at cause. Beliefs are generalisations about our own capability, and the way the world works. We talked in the last section about letting go of limiting beliefs, and installing better ones, and this is why that's

> *You are today where the thoughts of yesterday have brought you, and tomorrow you will be where the thoughts of today take you.*
>
> *Blaise Pascal*

important. If we are generalising information on the basis of unhelpful beliefs, then we are unlikely to be able to take advantage of opportunities. Beliefs are largely self-fulfilling prophecies. If we believe the world is a dangerous place, with everyone out to get us, then we will filter for that, and we will find it. However, if we believe in the intrinsic goodness in people – especially ourselves – then we will find that.

Even though our beliefs may be deeply ingrained, all they are really are habitual ways of thinking, and like any habit, they can be changed. They may be held at an unconscious level, but by becoming aware of them, we can change them, and begin to install more useful beliefs, that will lead to more empowering thinking patterns. You DO have power over your thoughts and beliefs!

Values

These work in two ways:

- ✓ They give us motivation

- ✓ They are the things we use to help us decide what is good and bad/ right and wrong

Values are often unconscious, which means you won't necessarily be aware of your values, and they are also different in different contexts. So what we might believe is important at work, may be quite different from what we think is important in relation to our kids. We are going to do an exercise looking at your values on page 127.

Preferences

We all have some in-born preferences. In NLP these are called *meta-programs*. They aren't right or wrong, they just are, and they don't change over the course of your lifetime. The main ones are a preference for:

✓ Introversion or extraversion

✓ Big picture or lots of detail

✓ Thinking or feeling

✓ Keeping options open or having things cut and dried

If we have an awareness of our preferences, we can then consciously learn the skills of the flip side of our preference. If we don't do this, then we may delete lots of opportunities as 'not for us'.

A personal example is that I have a preference for Introversion. This simply means that I draw my energy from having quiet reflective time, and I like to spend time with people on a one-to-one basis, and get to know them quite deeply. One of the skills in running a business though, is to be able to network extensively, with large numbers of people, and build more superficial relationships quickly. Initially, I deleted all opportunities that were presented to me to do this, as it just 'wasn't me', till my business coach pointed out to me that sometimes being 'not me' was exactly what a situation required. It's still not what I prefer to do, but I have learned the skill. So your preferences are just fine the way they are, but you do need to be aware of them, so that you can have a full range of options available to you.

Memories

Again, we talked about these a little in the previous section. Memories are a significant part of our back-story, and have often contributed to the formation of our beliefs. We will delete, distort and generalise on the basis of our memories, so in order for us to have more flexibility and options available to us, it is important to resolve our old memories, and use them as a resource.

Decisions

Before we develop a belief, we usually make a decision about ourselves or the world, often at a very young age. Because of this they are hard for us to access consciously. Nevertheless, limiting decisions made early in life will influence how we delete, distort and generalise. Perhaps when you were little you got a message that the world was a dangerous place, and perhaps that led you to decide that you couldn't cope if anything went wrong. Perhaps your mother was always telling you to 'take care' and 'be careful'. How different would it be if we were told to 'take some sensible risks today' instead?

Watch your language there!

There is no doubt that the words that we use in both our inner and outer conversations influences how we view the world, and ultimately how we think, feel and behave. It's another way in which we filter the world. Remember Susan, who described herself and her world as rubbish? And how her life began to change when she started to have different conversations with herself? Your language is simply the outward manifestation of your inner thoughts. Let's look at a few ways we can use language which will help or hinder us.

'Not bad' or 'pretty good'? The case for being positive

How often when you ask someone how they are do you get the response 'Not bad'. Not bad! The first problem with that phrase is that the unconscious mind does not process negatives particularly well. Let's do an example. I want you **not** to think of chocolate cake. In particular, I **don't want you to think** of a large slice of chocolate cake cut from a bigger cake, so that you can see the soft, gooey sponge and the layers of chocolate fondant cream sandwiching it together. And as you **don't think** of a slice of chocolate sponge cake, I certainly **don't want** you to be thinking of it with a sprinkle of icing sugar on the top, and a fork beside it, just waiting for you to **not** have a taste.

I once did this exercise with a group of student NLP practitioners, and at the break, one of the students ran to the bakery to buy some chocolate fudge cake, as no one could get the idea of eating the cake out of their mind. So in order to 'not' think of something, you need to first create an image of it, and then in some way attempt to erase it. So with 'not bad', you get a concept of bad, and then try to rub it out. But as you think of feeling bad, you immediately have a bit of an energy slump, as you will often need to actually access the feeling associated with it, before you can create it.

Problems or challenges

How often do you hear people say things such as 'The trouble with Mary is' or 'I've got a problem' or even 'What a disaster'? In our language, words like trouble and problem often bring to mind obstacles, barriers, things that we need to overcome in order to get anywhere. If I think about my 'problems' I feel exhausted before I even begin, at the thought of all the effort it is going to take to overcome them.

Challenges are something else though. Challenges are something I rise to. And even as I type that, I can feel my body shift in the chair, as I sit more upright, and feel more uplifted and energised.

Should, ought and must

These words all imply a lack of choice, and of necessity and compulsion. Words such as 'choose' 'could' and 'might', all imply choice and also promote the concept of being at cause. Even things which we believe we 'must' do are actually in reality choices. So while the motivation might be negative: 'I must go to work or I'll lose my job'; there is still a choice being made: it's better (for me) to go to work than lose my job.

The next exercise aims to give you some practice with using language in a way that gets you to cause, and emphasises choice over compulsion. Remember that even those things that appear to be necessities are still really choices.

Exercise: compulsion versus choice

In Table 3 on page 114 write a grumpy list. All the things you should do, must do, ought to do next week. What all your problems are. Go ahead, don't hold back, get it all out!

Now, how great do you feel after all that focus on these things you must do? Goodness, imagine having so many problems!

Bet you feel fantastic! Not. This time, remembering the concept of being at cause, go back and re-write everything in the second column, framed as a choice. Notice the difference in how you feel when you talk in this way? If you find yourself resisting this exercise, you might want to explore the extent to which you are at cause.

Table 3: compulsion versus choice

Grumpy list	Choice list
1.	
2.	
3.	
4.	
5.	
6.	
7.	
8.	
9.	
10.	

Can't or won't?

Often when people say they can't do something, they really mean they won't. I suspect it's because 'can't' seems slightly more polite. The problem with can't though, is that when you use it, you give your power away, and stop being at cause. 'Won't' keeps you at cause, and makes it clear that you have made a choice.

In the interests of good relationships, you may need to soften the delivery of 'won't' but the basis of all assertive communication is to be clear about your meaning. Imagine a friend asks you out for a drink. You've had a tiring day, and all you want to do is lie on the sofa watching television. However, because you don't want to offend her, you say 'I really can't tonight, I've got no babysitter/ the car has a flat tyre/ my shoe has a broken heel/ it's the week before payday'. You haven't been clear that you want to make a different choice and you may well find that your friend sets off to try and problem-solve these blocks for you. However, if you say clearly 'Thanks for the invite, I'm planning a night in tonight, I'm really tired', then you've been much clearer in what you mean, and in what you want.

Clients are often very keen to give me examples of what they can't do at this point. For example, they may say something like 'Well, I can't win a marathon at my age, can I?' I would still say that the issue is largely about won't. True, they may not be able to win a Gold Medal at the Olympics, but they could if they chose, get fit, start running, and do well for their age in a local marathon. They may choose not to do that as they don't enjoy it, or would rather spend time with their families at the weekends, or whatever. But it IS a choice. They could do it if they made different choices.

This can be uncomfortable, as suddenly people are faced with the prospects of no excuses!

Developing your inner optimist

The thing that always strikes me about filters is that with the exception of our in-born preferences, everything else is learned. This means that they can be unlearned! What would it be like if you could change these old murky grey filters for something different? What colours would your filters be? Brilliant blue? Cherry red? Sunshine yellow? Funky pink? You can choose to change what you pay attention to, what you distort, what you generalise, by just putting on a different set of filters.

> *Do, or do not do.*
> *There is no try.*
>
> *Yoda*

What would it be like to have an inner optimist that trusted that everything would be OK, and that even if it wasn't, that you would still cope? Sometimes the easiest way of doing this is just to try a new set of filters on for a week or two. Just decide what would be really strong, motivating, empowering stuff to have in there, and act 'as if' they were true. You've nothing to lose – after all, if you don't like that new positive optimistic you, you can always go back to the old one, can't you?

FIRST, SET YOUR SAT NAV

The first information your GPS navigation system needs when you ask it for directions is 'Where are you now?' Unless we know where we are starting from, most journeys would be impossible. On page 118 there is a useful and simple tool called the Wheel of Life which you can use to assess where you really are right at the moment.

Exercise: your Wheel of Life

Go round the wheel marking your current level of satisfaction within each area with 0 (right at the centre), being very low satisfaction and 10 (on the circumference) being fabulous. If any area doesn't apply to you at all, you can replace it with something else, but you should ensure that the wheel takes a holistic view of your life, covering physical, emotional, social and mental. Now join the dots. If you are like most people, your wheel will be pretty bumpy. Is it any wonder that life is feeling like it could be smoother? The great thing about the Wheel of Life is that you can now use your scores as a barometer to check your progress throughout your self-coaching.

Now decide which area is a priority for you to work on in the following exercises. Some people like to choose one that has a low score, others like to choose one that's nearly there. It doesn't actually matter which you start with, as you'll be working with them all eventually.

Figure 4: Wheel of Life

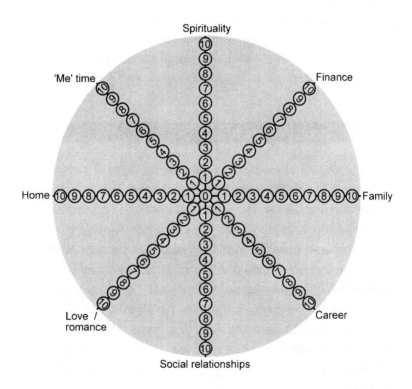

HOW HIGH UP THE LADDER ARE YOU?

In the previous chapter I talked about two women I had coached who had originally been sent by their companies for presentation and assertiveness skills coaching. The implication was that there was a skills and capability gap. A traditional approach would have been to have taken that at face value, and taught them a range of techniques aimed at effectively delivering and structuring a presentation or some assertiveness techniques. While this might have helped in the short term, longer term it would have been like only cutting the heads off a weed. It would have dealt with the visible outcome of their problem, but not the root cause, which would have quickly manifested itself again. So does this mean that skills training is never the answer? Absolutely not! One of these clients in particular had so successfully avoided presentations over the years that she did actually have a skills deficit, and after we had worked on the root cause of the problem, she was able to take advantage of a structured skill development programme. The point is that this alone would not have been adequate. Her root cause was based in a limiting belief she had about herself.

Case study: the problem wasn't where it seemed!

Graeme was another client who presented as having a skills deficit. He had been recently promoted, and was not performing to expectations in his new role. However, when I explained the concept of challenges having their root cause at different levels, it became apparent to Graeme that what he actually had was an identity level conflict: this new job no longer matched his view of himself, or his belief about his purpose in life. This level of dissonance at an identity level was challenging his values, his belief about himself, and manifesting as a capability issue.

The ladder on page 121 is based on work by Robert Dilts, who is one of the developers of NLP. He said that we can hold issues or challenges at any one of the levels on the ladder.

What tends to happen is that people will often work at too low levels when they are making changes, and so they don't tackle the root cause. Changing things low down the ladder won't influence higher levels, but changes made at the top will cascade downwards.

That is not to say that there is never a problem sitting solely at a lower level, but my advice is to always check. Otherwise you risk tinkering while Rome burns! This is exactly what I did personally in my earlier example about joining a fancy gym. I convinced myself that the reason I was not using the municipal gym, which was very cheap and within walking distance of my house, was that it wasn't a particularly nice environment. So I made a huge investment in changing the environment, to discover that the change really needed to happen at a values level. Our values help us evaluate what is important to us, and provide the juice to get us going. At that point in my life I had some values which demanded that I climb the corporate ladder and that motivated me to be in the office 12 hours most days. Going to the gym was a low value, low priority activity, no matter how pleasant the environment.

Figure 5: the change ladder

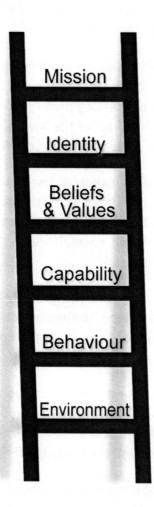

Exercise: how satisfied are you at each level?

Let's explore this more. Thinking of the priority area from your Wheel of Life, work through the following questions. This is not one that can be rushed, so allow yourself plenty of time for reflection. You can repeat the exercise for different contexts from your Wheel of Life. Record your thoughts about the questions in your journal.

- ✓ Environment: Where do you work and live? What external influences are there in your environment that you love? Which don't you like? Where would you like to be instead? What are the 'givens' that you feel are essential? To what degree do you have those?

- ✓ Behaviour: What do you do that you enjoy? What behaviour do you have that you would prefer not to have?   Do you behave in a way that supports how you want to be seen by yourself and the wider world? If not, what stops you?

- ✓ Capabilities: What are you good at? What new skills do you need to learn to support you in the context you are reflecting on? How would this contribute to you overall?

- ✓ Beliefs: What do you believe is true about you and those around you in the context you are thinking of? What would be a new and empowering belief to have in the context you are thinking of?

- ✓ Values: What is important to you about what you do? What factors influence your decisions?

- ✓ Identity/purpose: Who are you? Who are you not that you would like to be? What changes would need to take place to allow that to happen?

✓ Mission: What is the legacy you want to leave? How is what you are doing now going to contribute to that?

As with all the exercises, there is no one answer to these questions. However, I often find with clients that they have a sense of 'getting real' when they do this exercise. Many people begin to appreciate that their sense of 'there has to be more than this' is down to them fulfilling needs at the bottom of the ladder, at the expense of focusing on what really matters to them. This is why it's important for you to consider what success means to you.

SUCCESSORISE YOUR LIFE

Sadly, I often coach people who are asking themselves why they are so unhappy, when they have all the outward trappings of success. Often what has happened is that they have set out down a path littered with 'shoulds' and have ended up doing something they dislike, counting the days till they can retire. I have coached 40 year olds who talk about how many more years they will need to work before they can retire from a job they hate, and parents who are counting the years till their toddler goes to university so they can leave a relationship that is making them deeply unhappy. Is that how you are living your life?

> *I honestly think it is better to be a failure at something you love than to be a success at something you hate.*
>
> George Burns

Now clearly I'm not saying you need to make instant and irrevocable decisions here – sometimes thinking about how bad things are can be the impetus to make positive changes within the context you are in, rather than simply leaving it. And change of that magnitude usually requires careful planning and preparation, often with professional support.

It's really tough though to even start that process unless you have a clear idea of what it is you want instead. So the next exercise aims to help you work out what success would look, feel and sound like to you.

Exercise: what is success?

Look at your Wheel of Life again, and list in each segment what success looks like for you in that context. Ask yourself the following questions:

✓ What will I see when I'm successful in this context?

✓ What will I hear?

✓ What will I feel inside?

✓ What will I be saying to myself?

Be creative, this is your life – there is no need for you to conform to anyone else's indicators of success – not your parents, your peers, society at large. You have the choice here to set your own agenda. This is important before you get into goal setting.

WHAT'S THE VALUE?

If you were able to disengage from societal and peer group pressures, your answers to the previous exercise were probably driven by your values.

> *Open your arms to change, but don't let go of your values.*
>
> The Dalai Lama

More than anything, values are the things that have the most influence on your ability and willingness to change. They represent what is important to you. Values are those things that you are willing to invest time, energy and resources in, to achieve or avoid. They provide the kick-start motivation to do things, and you will use them to judge good and bad; right and wrong. Nevertheless, values are largely held at an unconscious level, and it's easy to ride rough-shod over them, and not notice until a sense of things not being right turns up. Identifying your values, and living your life guided by them is a means of being authentic and being the best that you can be.

Case study: a values conflict

Cameron had a value that said it was important to make a contribution, but his career was beginning to feel in conflict with this value. It was further complicated by another value that said that it was important for a man to provide for his family. (And for him, that meant good schools, holidays and so on.) Cameron came to coaching thinking that he might have to leave his job, and was in turmoil about the implications for the rest of his family. In fact, when he realised that there were two separate values conflicts happening, he decided he would volunteer at a youth club to support his value around contribution, while at the same time looking longer-term at his career and family roles.

Before you get into any goal setting, it's important for you to identify your own values, to ensure that your goals are aligned with them. In the future, this is a good exercise to do once a year, so that you check that your life planning is not veering away from your values. Too often we make grandiose New Year's Resolutions, and then don't follow through with them as they aren't aligned with our values, our identity or our mission in life.

Again, you might want to focus on one area or context from your Wheel of Life to do this exercise, and then come back and do the other segments at a later date.

Exercise: your values hierarchy

Using Table 4 on page 129, ask yourself the question 'What is important to me?' in the context you are thinking of. You will find that the first few come easily, as they will be held at a more conscious level, but keep asking 'and what else?' till you have at least 10. Write these in the left hand column of the table. Look at the list carefully, and see if there is anything missing.

Now you are going to rank them in order of importance. Ask yourself the questions:

✓ 'If I could only have one of these, which would it be?' Put a 1 in the second column, next to that value.

✓ Now ask yourself 'If I could have one more, which would it be?' Put a 2 next to that value in the second column.

Continue asking the question until you have all the values ranked. Resist the temptation to have lots that are 'equal'. I find clients always want to negotiate around that, but you will have a preference, even if very slight, for one over another. Remember that you are only thinking about one context at this stage.

In the third column, re-write your values in the order of importance, so you can see easily which the most important ones are.

Finally, in the right hand column, for each value, ask yourself the question:

✓ 'On a scale of one to 10, to what extent does what I do on a daily basis support these most important values?' Write the score for each value in the final column.

The answers will be useful to you when it comes to setting goals.

Table 4: what are your values?

What's important to me?	If I could only have one, which would it be?	Re-list values in order of importance	Extent to which I'm supporting these values with my daily actions?
1.			
2.			
3.			
4.			
5.			
6.			
7.			
8.			
9.			
10.			
11.			
12.			

WHAT'S YOUR PURPOSE?

Does your purpose in life revolve around getting to the end of the day or the week? Making it to your next holiday? If we are missing basic human needs for survival such as food, warmth or shelter; then finding those do become our purpose in life. However, most of us are fortunate enough not to be in that position, and yet once we no longer need to struggle every day to fulfil basic needs, many people find it hard to articulate what their purpose is..

> *Purpose serves as a principle around which to organise our lives.*
>
> *Anonymous*

Case study: lacking a sense of purpose

Katie came to see me after returning from a belated gap year. She had a first class degree and an MBA, and had been unable to find the sort of job she wanted, although by her own admission, she had no clue what that was. She had worked as an administrator in the public sector for a couple of years, before she felt she could no longer stand the boredom and lack of stimulation she was experiencing. A small legacy from an aunt gave her the means to take nine months out, which she had spent travelling. Her parents had funded coaching for her in an attempt to help her decide where her life was going. Katie felt completely stuck, and at the first session randomly suggested things that she 'might' do. After doing the exercise on page 131, it was clear that Katie's difficultly was at the life purpose level.

Purpose is about being rather than doing, and gets to the core of who you are. After exploring your life purpose, you will have a clearer idea of what you want, and what is really important to you. When you are fulfilling your life's purpose, people will often experience a sense of simply 'going with the flow'. Everything gets easier, and life becomes more enjoyable. Some people describe it as effortless. You may already have times in your life where you have this experience – imagine how great it would be if your whole life were to be lived like that.

This exercise has several stages and can take a two or three hours to do effectively, so you will probably want to spread it over a couple of days. I'd suggest that you allow yourself at least 30 minutes each time you work on it. You will find it useful to record it in your journal as you go along, so that you can refer back to it easily.

Exercise: your life purpose

When exploring your life purpose the first step is to identify words and phrases that resonate with you. Look at the list on page 134 and circle all the words that give you a good feeling when you think of them applied to you. If there are any which are important to you that are missing, then add them.

Notice if there are any themes emerging, and list them. In Katie's case, the themes that came out were autonomy and adventure.

The next step is to look for your motivational drivers. Ask yourself the following questions, ensuring you write the answers down. Write quickly, record whatever comes up, and be honest. No one else is going to read this. Do it with a light heart!

✓ What makes you smile? (This might be anything from people, hobbies, activities)

✓ Throughout your life, what activities have consistently brought you happiness and joy?

✓ What activities absorb you so much you lose track of time?

✓ What is unique about you?

✓ What makes you feel proud of yourself?

✓ What qualities in other people do you most aspire to?

✓ What are you naturally good at? What are your skills, abilities and gifts?

✓ What do people typically ask you for help in?

✓ If you had to teach something, what would you teach, and who would you reach out to?

✓ What would you regret not fully doing, being or having in your life?

✓ What are your most important values, from the values exercise on page 127?

✓ What challenges and difficulties have you overcome?

✓ What resources did you use to do this?

✓ What are you passionate about?

Take some time to review your answers to the previous questions, and then answer these questions:

- ✓ How can you use your talents, passions and values to live the life you want?

- ✓ What will you see, hear and feel when you are doing so?

- ✓ What will others say about you?

- ✓ What is the very first thing you need to do to move you towards this?

- ✓ When will you do it?

You are now ready to start putting it all together by writing your purpose statement. For this part of the exercise, I suggest you make yourself comfortable somewhere, either indoors or out, and set yourself a time limit. Twenty minutes is usually enough to start with. Take the information you've gained from the earlier part of the exercise, and use the combination of words and phrases to come up with your personal statement of purpose, that has most meaning for you. For that 20 minutes, just write continuously. No editing - just let it out. You can refine it later.

Once you have your statement in draft form, put it away for a week or so, and then refine it further. It will be useful for you to have in mind when you are working through the final chapters of this book.

Key words and phrases list

Personal achievement

Happiness

Money

Loving someone

Being loved

Being popular

Competence

Independence

Taking risks

Being your best

Reaching your potential

Finding excitement

Being a leader

Continuous learning

Being excellent

Making a contribution

Being free to express yourself

Making a positive difference

Becoming an expert

Seeing how much you can get away with

Winning

Interdependence (working with others)

Working with detail

Finding the good in others

Gaining recognition

Creating something

Gaining approval

Getting things done

Doing good

Dominating

Being unique

Being the best

Gaining security or safety

Controlling

Having fun

Working hard

Having influence

Experiencing life to the fullest

Seeking adventure

Power and authority

Prestige

Increasing effectiveness

Having lots of options

Having a plan

Having time and space

Sparking off other people

Being strategic

ASK BETTER QUESTIONS
AND GET BETTER ANSWERS

We are now almost two thirds of the way through this book, and I'm wondering what your inner voice is saying to you? What assumptions are you making about yourself, and about the tools and techniques that you now have at your fingertips?

If you are completely revved up and ready to go, then fantastic. You are almost ready to plan for the most fabulous future.

Or are you feeling that this might work for other people? That it's not really 'you'? What assumptions are you still making about yourself? That you aren't smart enough, clever enough, pretty enough, thin enough, young enough, rich enough? I wonder how these assumptions would stand up to a good reality check?

Are you asking yourself a lot of 'why?' questions? People often think 'why' is a good thing to ask to get answers, but that is often not the case. 'Why' questions are often not that useful. 'Why' tends to push us back to effect, and back into our stories. We look for excuses, reasons and justifications, rather than answers. When I did my very first NLP training, there were big notices all over the room saying 'Never ask why!' And when I frequently did, as it had been a favourite counselling question of mine, the trainer would shoot across the room (I'm convinced he had some sort of robotic ears that scanned the room for that word), and with increasing levels of frustration ask me, yet again, to stop.

Children ask 'why' a lot. When my daughter was little, she went through that phase of asking 'why?' several times an hour. 'Why' is about wanting to understand, and to make sense of how the world works. However, once we've created that sense of order, then why becomes more about making sense of the past, and if there are no answers (and there often aren't) then we can be left feeling stuck, frustrated, and unable to move on. 'Why' takes us back into emotion, and often has us looking for blame and fault.

Clearly I'm making a bit of a generalisation here, and some people will feel very strongly that they can't move on till they have answers to the 'why' question. However, that question tends to belong more in therapy than coaching. If the 'why' questions won't go away for you, and you find yourself unable to move on, you might want to consider counselling or therapy rather than coaching. You can find details of organisations that can help you at the back of the book.

Even 'why' questions that superficially appear to be useful might not be the right question. If I ask 'Why did I get a blank screen when I pressed that button my keyboard?' I don't really want someone to explain to me what is going on in the depths of my laptop when I press a particular button. What I actually want to know is 'What do I need to do to get it to produce the result I want?' and possibly 'What does that original button actually do?'

So if I were to ask you 'Why are you so unhappy?' you would give me a lot of information from your past that had led to your current unhappiness. You would possibly go back and live those occasions again in your mind, and make yourself feel even worse. However, if I were to ask you a range of 'what' questions that would move you forward. For example, 'What do you need to do in order to let go of this unhappiness?' is a completely different kind of question. It opens up the potential for change - that you will feel happy again - and it sets you off looking for solutions.

This is not to say that your reasons for being unhappy aren't legitimate ones, but what I am saying is that to continually return to 'Why did that happen to me' is going to keep you stuck in the past, looking for reasons. When you want to move on, you need a different set of questions.

'Who, why, where, how', can all be what I call 'gossipy' questions, designed to elicit more and more detail, and drive people further into their stories – and other people's stories can be quite fascinating. I do a lot of my writing in coffee shops, and I love to people-watch. Last week, two young women were sitting next to me, and one had clearly just ended a relationship with her partner. As she told the story, her friend asked frequent questions: 'Why did he say that? Where were you? Who started the row? When is he coming for his stuff?' In response, the other woman provided a blow by blow account of the entire row, and I did find myself leaning nearer to them in order to hear every detail. Even I was hooked into the drama, but I couldn't help but think if she had just asked her friend 'What support do you need' or 'What needs to happen now?' it would have been more helpful and moved her friend from problem to solutions.

People who have a preference for feeling over thinking are more likely to continue to seek information. Their motivation for this is that they tend to want to really understand the problem subjectively, and it is done with the best of intentions. This can be particularly useful in the early stages of any sort of crisis, when de-briefing can be exactly what you need to do, but it is rarely useful to stay in that place too long. When you begin to ask yourself 'what' questions, then you shift your thinking to future, and to solution. It's a completely different frame. You rarely need to fully understand a problem to be able to fix it.

One of the nicest things a client can say to me is 'That's a good question', so I suggest you get some practice in asking yourself better questions, so that you can coach yourself more effectively. Good questions will liberate you! There is no place to hide with 'what'. Ask yourself what, and you give yourself the message that you believe in yourself enough to know that you can sort the problem out.

Exercise: moving to solution focused thinking

Use Table 5 on page 141 for this exercise. Think of all the 'why' questions you ask yourself, and make a list below. I've put in a few to start you off – score them out if they aren't relevant. In the second column, write a more empowering question, based around 'what'. Now this isn't just about semantics – you really need to shift your focus from problem to solution with this exercise.

Table 5: asking better questions

What are you currently saying?	What are you going to say instead?
Why is this happening to me?	What do I need to do to get through it?
Why am I so miserable?	
Why don't I have any friends?	
Why did I get ill?	
Why am I such a waste of space?	

GETTING PEOPLE ON SIDE

Sometimes we have people in our life who don't support us, and we talked in the previous chapter about how it is sometimes necessary to let the relationship go if it continues to hold you back. Of course, you will have many more relationships where you really want to improve the communication with the other person. This is especially important when you are making big changes in your life, and you really want to understand the impact on someone else.

Or maybe you have someone in your life that you simply don't see eye to eye with? Someone who, no matter how hard you try, you just keep banging up against? If it is in the best interests of you both to resolve the difficulties between you, then the following exercise can be a powerful method of improving communication.

> **Never judge another until you have walked a mile in their moccasins**
>
> *Native American Proverb*

One important point before you do this exercise is to ensure that it is appropriate for you to have a better understanding and relationship with the other person. So if, for example, you have experienced abuse or violence towards you, then I wouldn't recommend that you use this, as you do not have to hear the other person justifying their actions to you. In that situation, I would suggest you work with a professional. Details of organisations that can help are at the back of the book.

Case study: walking in someone else's shoes

Marie was desperately worried about her teenage daughter. She had a boyfriend who Marie considered completely unsuitable, and she was terrified that her daughter would become pregnant and drop out of education. She had tried to have a discussion with her daughter on several occasions, but it had always ended in a screaming and shouting match. After she commented several times that 'She just didn't know what was going on inside her daughter's head', I suggested we do this exercise.

During the exercise Marie gained the perspective that her daughter felt her privacy was being invaded, and that she was not being trusted by her mother. She checked this assumption out with her daughter directly, and the fact that her mother now seemed to really understand her perspective made her daughter open up about the worries she had about her relationship with the young man. Suddenly mum and daughter were back on the same side.

Exercise: it's good to talk

This fly-on-the-wall technique is based on work done by Judith DeLozier and John Grinder. Its great strength is that it helps you to answer that question of 'What on earth is going on in their head?' It also allows you to look at the dynamic between you and the other person. Read it through a couple of times to ensure you understand it, but it is fine to use the book as a prompt as you work through the exercise. It involves you taking up three positions:

✓ First position: you are you. You look at the world from your perspective, and get to put forward your own point of view. You are speaking from your own perspective, describing how the situation seems to you.

✓ Second position: you metaphorically step into the other person's shoes, and tell the same story from their perspective. You consider how it would look, feel and sound to them. You really need to focus on getting inside the other person's head at this position. If you find yourself saying 'I'm obviously completely unreasonable, and the other person is right, and we'll do it their way', then that is still your first person wishful thinking! Be honest about what you really think the other person is thinking and feeling about the situation.

✓ Third position: you get to be a fly on the wall. You look at the dynamic happening between the other two people. You have no emotional investment in either 'winning'. In this position you simply notice what is happening. Your job in this position is to generate and evaluate some useful choices in a difficult situation.

Although it is possible to do this exercise 'in your head', most people find it more powerful to actually move from chair to chair as they move into the different positions, and to talk aloud. The position of the chairs is shown below. Two should be angled and quite close to each other, the third should be further away and facing the other two

Figure 6: chair arrangement for 'It's good to talk'

This is what you do:

✓ Get an item such as a cushion or jacket that can sit in the first chair throughout, to represent you.

✓ Sit in the first chair, and pretend the person you have the difficulty with is sitting in the chair next to you. Describe the problem to them from your perspective. If you have anything you want to say directly to the other person, do so now. Get it all out! When you feel you have said everything you want to say, move into the next chair, leaving behind the cushion or jacket to represent an imaginary you still sitting there.

✓ Sit in the second chair as the other person in the problem relationship. Tell the problem again from THEIR perspective, speaking to the cushion that you have left in the first chair to represent the real you. Again, if there is anything you want to say to the imaginary you in the first chair from your position as the OTHER person, do so. When you have told the story, move into the third chair.

✓ Sit in the third chair as the fly on the wall. Offer the imaginary you sitting in the first chair anything you have noticed about the dynamic, their behaviour, voice tone, posture, phrasing etc. Offer any advice that would seem helpful. Remember you cannot influence the other person's responses with these observations, only the responses of the imaginary you.

✓ Go back and sit in the first chair again as you, and think about the learning you have had, and what you are going to do differently from now on.

✓ If you need to, you can go round the cycle again. Always end in position one.

THROWING BALLS IN THE AIR
AND HOPING THEY DON'T FALL

At this point in coaching, lots of people start fretting about how much time they need to find: time to honour their core values and find their life purpose, while still holding down a job, being a taxi service for the kids, never mind shopping, eating, sleeping, maintaining a relationship and housework. However, I don't see this as a time management issue, I see it as a priority management one.

A useful metaphor is to imagine for a minute that your life is like a bucket. It has a finite amount of space. In that bucket you need to place some stones, each of which represents some key priority for you. You also need to fit in some gravel, which might be maintenance type things (shopping, cooking), and some sand – just trivia, basically. The sand might represent time spent watching TV that you aren't really that interested in, surfing the net, using chat rooms. And then some water – go with the flow time.

How we choose to fill the bucket represents our priorities. We can't actually change the bucket, but we can change the order in which we put things in. If we fill it with sand and gravel first, then you won't be able to force the big stones in – it's as if the other stuff creates an impermeable barrier. However, if the big stones go in first, then usually we can squeeze in enough water, sand and gravel round about them – in fact the bucket that looked full actually has a lot of spare capacity.

Writing this book had been a dream of mine for years. Every New Year's Eve, I would promise myself that this would be the year I would do it. And another year would pass, and it still wouldn't be done. The reason for that was that I never promoted it to the level of being a stone. So once I had filled my bucket of life up with other stuff, there was no room for it. And then the year came when I decided 'This year, it becomes a stone, and it goes in the bucket first'. And suddenly, in my over-stuffed diary, time just miraculously appeared to do it. Yes, we had more dust for a few weeks. And my internet friendships took a bit of a bashing. But everything important still got done (so long as I promoted them to a big stone, and put them in the bucket first), AND the book got written.

Exercise: defining your priorities

Make a list of your big stones: what are your dreams? What is really important to you in relation to all the segments in your Wheel of Life? Once you've identified them get them in your diary.

What are the bits of gravel: the routine 'keeping body and soul together' stuff that we all need to do? Fit them round your big stones in your diary.

List the bits of sand: what are the total time-wasters in your life? Be honest with yourself. What would you be prepared to let go in order to make room for your big stones? Are you really going to be lying on your death bed mourning the fact that you missed that reality TV programme? But would you be sorry not to have done your big stones in life?

Finally, we are human – life isn't an exact science, so leave some room for the 'go with the flow' stuff.

After you've done this exercise, the rest is about developing some good habits.

The illustration below gives you an idea about how this works – and you can start your year anytime!

Figure 7 : managing your priorities

On a weekly basis, fit the gravel and sand around the big stones, ensuring you leave some flexibility for those opportunities that suddenly present themselves.

Every year, take a broad brush look at what you want to achieve in relation to each aspect of your Wheel of Life. These are your big stones.

Every month, identify exactly what you are going to do which will contribute to you achieving your big stones, and fit this into your diary.

Remember – being busy all the time isn't enough, if you are busy doing the wrong things. Get into the habit of recognising what the right things are for you. It's about working smarter, not harder.

RELAX AND BREATHE:
RELEASE STRESS AND HEAL YOUR BODY

Do you ever feel that you run fast all day in order to simply stay still? It seems to be one of realities of modern life for many people, but it doesn't have to be like that. The activities in the previous section will help a lot with helping you to identify the really important stuff, so that you can give yourself permission to let some the other stuff go, at least for now. Nevertheless, many people have felt stressed for so long, that they need some specific techniques to allow them to relax.

> *The more tranquil a person becomes, the greater is their success, their influence, their power for good. Calmness of mind is one of the beautiful jewels of wisdom.*
>
> *James Allen*

Physical and emotional stress becomes intertwined, and in order to let go of emotional stress, we need to learn first to let go of physical tension. While a degree of stress can be useful, when we become over-stressed, a whole range of physical and mental complaints follow, affecting every system of our body. Look at the picture on page 151 to see the sorts of problems caused by stress. Additionally there is evidence that long term stress increases the risk of some cancers, some types of heart disease, and strokes.

Researchers in the field of neuro-science have discovered that meditation actually changes the brain. Dr David Hamilton, in his amazing book called *How Your Mind Can Heal Your Body* describes a study carried out in New England in 2005, which showed that regular meditation increased the thickness of the pre-frontal cortex of the brain, the area that controls concentration, freewill and compassion. So it appears that when you do visualisation exercises, you may actually be changing the microscopic structure of the brain. This is exciting stuff, and means that visualisation is not just a nice thing to do for half an hour, but actually causes chemical and structural changes in the brain. Now wouldn't that be worth learning?

Figure 8: A picture of stress

A: headaches
B: blurred vision
C: difficulty swallowing and dry mouth
D: aching neck and shoulder muscles
E: over-breathing and palpitations
F: high blood pressure and heart disease
G: diarrhoea, nausea, indigestion and ulcers
H: tremors
I: pins and needles and cold extremities
J: skin rashes and some eczemas
K: some cancers

Repair, regenerate, rejuvenate!

The following exercise is designed to help you heal and repair both your mind and your body. You should allow 30 minutes to do it, and you might find that it helps initially if you record it on your computer or on a tape, so that you can just relax and listen. Speak slowly and in a calm, gentle voice, leaving lots of gaps. Alternatively, read it through a couple of times, and trust that your unconscious mind will know what to do – because it does! You can do the exercise either sitting or lying, but I tend to find I fall asleep if I do meditation lying down. However, whatever works best for you is fine.

Exercise: healing meditation

Find yourself somewhere comfortable, where you won't be disturbed. If you want, take your shoes off, and loosen tight waistbands. You might find that your body temperature drops when you are very relaxed, so it's a good idea to have a light blanket to hand.

Close your eyes, and take a few slow deep breaths in and out. If you need to change your position at any time, then do so. Notice if your breath is going right the way down to your tummy. If not, then allow yourself to breathe right down into your abdomen, so that your tummy rises and falls with each breath. As you notice your breathing, notice the sensation as the air enters your nose..... trace that sensation down to your lungs..... notice your abdomen rising. Now notice it in reverse as you breathe out.....

Take your attention outside yourself for a moment..... silently say to yourself what you are aware of through any of your senses. For example, 'I am aware of the traffic noises in the distance. I am aware of the sun of my face. I am aware of the smell of something cooking'. Simply notice what you notice.....

Now turn your attention inwards again. Let the parts of your body come into awareness in any order..... what did you notice first.....? What part next.....? Notice the internal sensations. Perhaps you can feel your breath moving in..... and out..... or perhaps you can notice a pulse somewhere..... or perhaps the sensation in your abdomen of food being digested..... or perhaps just a feeling..... of peace..... and relaxation.

Turn your attention outwards again. What do you notice this time? Perhaps the sound of children, playing..... in the distance..... or of an aeroplane, far overhead..... take a few minutes to notice what it is you notice.

And again, now, turn inwards. Compare the right side of your body to the left side..... do you notice any difference?

And outwards again, what do you notice......

Back again to your body. Are you aware of any sensations in your body? Just notice. If you had to describe this sensation, what would you say? What is the texture and colour of it? Where is it located? Is it warm, or cool? Does it have a shape? What size is it? Are there any sounds or pictures associated with the sensation? As you pay complete attention to it, notice if it changes..... what happens to it? Let your body do whatever it seems to want to do, as you sit there quietly for the next few minutes.....

Now imagine that you could become infinitesimally small. So small that you can follow the breath all the way round your body, passing right into your blood cells, and visiting every part of you. And on each circuit round your body, notice if there is anything that you need to clean up..... anything you need to let go..... check if there is any disease, or pain or discomfort anywhere, and allow it to become bathed in healing light. The light can wash around your body. I wonder what colour your light is? As you clean up the inside of your body, bathing it in healing light, you can perhaps notice if there is anything else you need to do, right now.....You don't need to, understand how your body works. You simply need to trust that your unconscious mind knows what to do, and ask it now to return you to the blueprint for total health. Just ask.....

At any time in the future that you need to, you can allow your body to become bathed in light, and for every cell and nerve to become whole and healthy.

Now as you rest there, you might want to imagine yourself in a place outdoors where you feel calm and comfortable and serene. It could be a beach, or a wood, or a park..... or even your own garden..... or simply your own doorstep. Be there now.....

Notice the sensation of the air on your face. Is it warm or cool, in this special place of yours? As you rest there quietly, allow a cloud to appear on the horizon. It's just a light, fluffy cloud, almost insubstantial. Like wisps of cotton wool, high, high above you.....

Simply watch, with a sense of curiosity, as that cloud drifts overhead. This cloud has come to do you a special service. It can take any worries, negativity or anxieties. It has an infinite capacity to absorb, to neutralise and clean everything up, making it completely safe, before letting them go, far out over the sea, like soft and gentle rain. Watch as one by one, your anxieties release themselves. Some may drift up to the cloud, slowly....lazily. Others may race upwards, realising completely that it is time for them to go. That you no longer need them..... and as you watch, the cloud can become heavier and denser...... does it change colour..... or shape....?

Observe peacefully, as the cloud begins to move away..... moving slowly to begin with and then perhaps picking up speed..... going off into the distance..... into the far, far horizon, taking everything you no longer need with it, so that you can be calm, and relaxed now.

Now I want to tell you a story, a story about a giant redwood tree. These trees are amazing. They can withstand anything. They have deep, deep, roots..... and those roots nurture it, and support it, and ensure that the tree has everything it needs to be strong.....

As well as pushing downwards, into the soil, the tree reaches upwards to the sky. Always knowing that anything is possible. That new growth is possible, even if, further down, it once had injuries. It can repair itself, and heal, and grow.....

Finally, as well as having deep steadying roots, and pushing towards the energy from the sun, getting resources from many places, redwood trees reach out to each other. Under the soil, the roots of the trees become entwined, so that in stormy times, they can support each other..... while in the sky, the branches also entwine together, as if holding hands. On one side, supporting..... and on the other side being supported.

Ask yourself, 'Is that balance of supporting and being supported right in my life, right now?' And if not, ask your unconscious mind to support you, in finding a way to be completely balanced......

If at any time in the future you need to, you can go back to this exercise, simply by focussing on your breathing, and by thinking about a healing light..... and a cloud...... and a tree, with many resources.

So for now, it's time to come back to full awareness, knowing that you are resilient and strong, and that you have many, many resources.

Become aware of your breathing, and how you are sitting or lying. Begin to gently move your arms and legs. Still staying in that relaxed state, slowly turn your attention outwards again, and notice what you notice. What do you hear? What do you feel?

When you are ready, open your eyes, have a big stretch and a yawn, and come back fully into the present moment.

How did you feel after doing that exercise? It's not uncommon to feel a little spacey initially when you do relaxation exercises - you may have been more relaxed than you have been for months. I suggest you make some kind of meditation and relaxation exercise a big stone in your life, at least three times a week, if not more.

Once you become comfortable with the process, you can adapt it to add your own suggestions in. If you are looking for ideas for symbols or metaphors that can be helpful, here are some ideas that my students have shared with me.

Letting go can be symbolised by:

- ✓ Burning problems in a grate

- ✓ Tying problems to a helium balloon

- ✓ Washing them down a plug hole

- ✓ Writing a letter

- ✓ Watching snow melt in the spring

- ✓ Having a shower in healing light

- ✓ Allowing things to become transparent

- ✓ Tearing paper in the wind

- ✓ Feathers being caught in a breeze

Getting new resources can by symbolised by:

- ✓ Trees

- ✓ Animals

- ✓ The sun rising in the morning

- ✓ The moon waxing and waning

- ✓ Diamonds

- ✓ Mythological creatures

- ✓ Celebrities or people from history

You might want to record in your journal some ideas for your own visualisations. Remember these simple guidelines:

- ✓ What you think about affects your body – your emotional thoughts are the weather your body has to live in – you choose whether your weather is winter or summer.

- ✓ You tend to get what you expect, via the filtering process.

- ✓ The hardest part about changing is getting started - once you have started to change, your mind becomes open to new possibilities, and subsequent change becomes easier.

- ✓ Your unconscious doesn't need to be 'forced' to change – just ask it to do so, and expect that it will.

First-aid measures for the soul

Have you ever been at a family gathering, and you feel stressed out of your mind? Or been in the middle of a difficult meeting at work, and just wanted to scream? Or listened to your children squabbling and just wanted to run away? While I can't emphasise enough the long term benefits of regular visualisation and meditation, sometimes you do just need a quick fix to get you back in touch with yourself in tough situations. I have done the following exercise on tube trains, in the toilet in the middle of difficult meetings, and in the kitchen at home. In fact anywhere

where you can be by yourself for two or three minutes! It's an ideal tool to get you back on top.

Exercise: two minute chill-out

Find a spot where you can be by yourself – if you can sit down, that's easiest, but you can do this standing up as well.

Take a slow, deep breath in, and as you exhale, allow your eyes to close.

While continuing to breathe slowly, in through your nose, and out through your mouth, you are going to quickly scan key areas of your body, tensing and releasing as you do so.

First, notice your shoulders. As you breathe in, tense them up even more; then as you breathe out, let your shoulders move down, and back, till they are completely relaxed.

Now move your attention to your forehead, and while breathing in, draw the muscles in your forehead into a frown, and as you breathe out, let them relax.

Do the same with the muscles in your jaw, ensuring that when you breathe out, your jaw is relaxed, and your teeth are slightly parted in your mouth.

With the next breath out, check that your shoulders are still relaxed.

Finally, clench your hands as you breathe in, and then relax them as you breathe out.

Take three more, deep, slow breaths, in through your nose and out through your mouth. Imagine that you are breathing in a cool, calm light of relaxation, and as you breathe out, you blow away clouds of stress and tension.

When you feel ready, open your eyes.

PROGRAMME IN YOUR DESTINATION

At the beginning of this chapter, I talked about setting your sat nav with a review of where you currently are in your life. We're going to end it now with an exercise which will help you programme in your destination.

> *'Would you tell me please which way I ought to go from here?', said Alice*
>
> *'That depends on where you want to go', said the Cat*
>
> *'I don't much care where', said Alice*
>
> *'Then it doesn't much matter which way you go', said the Cat*
>
> *Lewis Carroll: Alice's Adventures in Wonderland*

Exercise: what is your end goal?

Find a quiet spot to do this exercise, where you can be undisturbed. If it helps, do the chill-out mediation on page 159 as a means of helping you relax and focus.

Imagine for a moment that it's your 85th birthday party. Be there, look down at your hands, notice the skin – is it thinner than now – perhaps you have some age spots? Notice how you are sitting or standing. Look around, and notice who is there – maybe friends, children and grandchildren, who you haven't even met yet? These people are all here with you to celebrate a long life, well lived.

One by one your loved ones stand up and speak about you. What do you want them to say? What do you want to hear? How do you want to feel? What do you want your legacy to the world to be? How do you want friends, family, work colleagues to remember you? And then ask yourself two questions:

- ✓ 'What am I doing right now, that is moving me towards that reality?'

- ✓ 'If I continue on the path I'm currently on, will I create that reality?'

This can be a tough exercise, and one that sometimes causes high emotions in people. Remind yourself that there are options here – you can choose a different path now, today, and create the reality you want, out there in your future.

Someone who managed to change his end goal very effectively was Alfred Nobel. Nobel had an opportunity few of us have – a newspaper prematurely published his obituary, and Nobel saw himself described as the Angel of Death for his invention of dynamite. He realised that was not how he wanted to be remembered by the world, and so he left almost his entire estate to fund the establishment of five prizes, including the Nobel Peace Prize.

It is never too late to start working towards the end goal you want.

Record your learning from this exercise in your journal.

CHECKPOINT

If you've got this far in the book, you are doing great, and you are now ready to look at how to create a fabulous future for yourself.

In this section, you've learned:

✓ How you delete, distort and generalise information based on what is in your filters, and how to do so in more useful ways.

✓ How to use a Wheel of Life to assess where you are at the moment, and to use it as a barometer for change

✓ How to assess which level you are holding a challenge at, using the ladder of change

✓ How to use language in more empowering ways and to ask better questions of yourself

✓ What your purpose is

✓ How to align your values

✓ A technique for improving relationships

✓ How to prioritise

✓ Visualisation and meditation

✓ How to start with the end in mind

Give yourself a huge pat on the back for getting this far. Check in with your inner cheerleader on a regular basis, and remember to keep your journal.

Now to the future and beyond - see you in the next section!

5

CREATING A
FABULOUS FUTURE

ROUTE PLANNER

This section is FUN! Now you have put your support system in place, cleared the ground for change and learned how to live authentically in the present, this is the place where you begin to be the creator of your own future. You may in the past have felt that you were driven by your circumstances in life, but now you will begin to explore how you can be driven by choices.

Would you like to set some bold, inspiring goals for yourself? This section will show you how. You will learn the seven powerful beliefs of successful people and how to instantly motivate yourself. You will even do some time travel, so that by the end of this section, your new goals will be firmly installed in your future, drawing you irresistibly towards them.

EXERCISES IN THIS SECTION

What are my habits?	30 minutes
What would you do?	30 minutes
Getting to goals	30 minutes
Happy buttons	15 minutes
Swish that goal!	10 minutes
Drawing your road-map	20 minutes
Exploring the future	20 minutes

THE FOUNDATIONS FOR SUCCESS

What do you believe?

What makes some people successful at what they do? I don't mean what makes some people rich. That may be one measure of success, but I've never been the type of coach that measures my own or my clients' success in terms of what they have. For me, success is about living a life that honours your core values.

So what sorts of beliefs do happy successful people have in their filters? Have a look at the list below.

> When you face the sun, the shadow will always lie behind you.
>
> *Helen Keller*

I know myself better than anyone else in the world

People who have this belief tend to tune in fairly easily to their inner wisdom. For some this is an intuitive process, and for others it is fairly structured. Gavin described it to me like this "I imagine that I have inside me lots of different parts with different skills and knowledge. When I need to make a big decision, I imagine them all having a meeting, and coming up with some answer". This is very similar to the Board of Directors exercise we talked about on page 43. Essentially, Gavin was using his imagination to access his unconscious resources. You can do this too.

I already have all the resources I need to succeed in this situation

It's all too easy to put off action until you have more money, lose weight, get a new car or house, get the kids independent. But you know what - there will always be a reason not to. You may not yet have exactly the material resources or skills that you need to make the change – but you do have the resources to get them if you need them. People who are living the life of their dreams have the confidence of believing that they have knowledge, skills and experience in abundance, and if they need anything, they will find it.

If something seems hard, then I can chunk it down into small steps

It's the old adage – how do you eat an elephant? One bite at a time. Or a journey of thousand miles starts with a single step. Some of us have a preference for looking at the big picture, and others will prefer starting with detail. If you are a big picture person, it can be easy to feel a little overwhelmed. I have a big picture preference, so every time I thought about writing this book, all I could see was the phrase 'Fifty Thousand Words', flashing in glorious techno-colour right in front of my eyes. Then I would get panic stricken, and list all the reasons it couldn't get done. I'd never see my daughter. I would never go out with my husband again. I would never do any washing, cooking or cleaning. My business would disappear. So I would put the dream aside again. Then one day, I was walking the dog, and I got to thinking about how many words I might write in a normal day: when I totted up my blog, emails, Facebook, Twitter, I estimated that I was already writing about 2000 words. This provided me with some evidence – I already knew I could do that easily enough. I made a promise to myself that at least 5 days a week I would sit down and write 2000 words. I never thought beyond that. All I had to write was 2000 words. Easy – I was already doing it, after all. And it **was** easy. So think of the dreams you have, and break them down into more manageable pieces. While

I'm all for a bit of stretch and challenge, don't set yourself up to fail. Much better to feel pride every day at what you have achieved, than beat yourself up for the things you didn't do.

If what I'm doing isn't working I'll do something else

If you always do what you've always done, you'll always get what you've always got! In NLP, we describe this in terms of being aware and responsive to feedback we receive via our senses of sight, hearing, feelings, touch, taste and smell. Are you getting feedback that your actions are moving you towards your goals?. Does this give you a good feeling? What do you hear people saying about this? If the feedback you get is that it's not moving you towards what you want, then simply change it. OK, it may set you back a little, but better to do something different now, than be stuck with an end result you don't want. Remember what I told you earlier about Marion, who within weeks of her first panic attack had agoraphobia so severely she was confined to one room? The comfort zone shrinks so easily and rapidly when we don't take action to keep pushing it outwards.

I have many small-business people as friends. They have all been feeling the squeeze of the recent recession. Some have sadly gone to the wall. They tended to be the ones who worked harder and harder within the same business model that served them in the past. The ones who have survived have adapted quickly to current circumstances and adopted new ways of working. Not only have they survived, but many of them have thrived.

Case study: daring to be different

Derek was a team leader in a large organisation. He was desperate to prove himself, and took a hard management line with his staff, adhering strictly to the rule book, and allowing them little scope for initiative. The more his staff challenged this regime, the more entrenched Derek became in it, increasing his degree of micro-management on a weekly basis. He started to notice a pattern of sabotage and lack of cooperation amongst his team, which he took as a sign that he needed to manage them even more closely.

Derek was given feedback at an appraisal that the company was beginning to consider that they had made a recruitment error with him, and he was asked to attend coaching in an attempt to develop his management style.

Through doing many exercises like the ones in this book, and inviting 360 degree feedback from his peers, managers and staff, Derek came to the realisation that something had to change. He wasn't sure what initially, and was worried that if he relaxed his management style everything would fall apart. However he decided to take some controlled risks and give his staff more latitude. Within weeks he started to see a change in their behaviour, as they also began to feel empowered and enabled to do the job they were employed to do with some creativity.

Exercise: what are my habits?

Ask yourself:

- ✓ 'What do I habitually do?'

- ✓ 'Does that bring me the results I want?'

- ✓ 'What could I do differently that MIGHT bring me the results I want?' (Remember that there is no failure, only feedback.)

Nearly always in order to see change, you have to take some risks, and do something different. Thinking this way gives you some choices about how you behave, and it also assists you to stay at cause. Sometimes maintaining the status quo is the worst possible outcome. Phrases such as 'That's the way we've always done it around here' or 'If it ain't broke, don't fix it' can be the death knell to any sort of creativity and change.

> **The future belongs to those who believe in the beauty of their dreams.**
>
> *Eleanor Roosevelt*

Remember, people come to coaching because they either want to stop doing something, or start doing something. I'm sure you didn't buy this book because you were saying to yourself 'My life is just perfect, and there is nothing in it I want to change, so I will buy this book to learn how to stay completely static'. Did you?

So in order to create this great future that is out there waiting for you, you need to start doing some things differently. Starting now! There is a solution to every problem if you are prepared to look for it. Just doing one small thing differently every day can mount up to massive change. As these changes happen, you will notice that new options will appear, doors will begin to open, and you will start to see different results.

There is no such thing as failure

I often ask my clients what they would do if they knew they could not fail. When you ask that question, you often get to the very core of someone's dreams. So let's just dump that entire concept of failure. Have you ever had an old picture, and it's been on the wall for years, and then one day, for some reason, you take it down, clean and it and put a new frame on it? Although the picture hasn't changed, it looks completely different with the new frame. What I want you to do, right now, is to put a new frame around failure. A failure is just a result – perhaps a different one from the one you expected, but still a result. Learn from it, and move on. The only real failure is to not learn from what happens.

How would your life change if that was a belief about the world that you held in your filters?

Thomas Edison took a long time to invent the first light bulb. Rumour has it that he made over 2000 experiments to perfect it. At the press conference to launch his new invention, a pushy journalist put the knife in: 'Say, Mr. Edison, how did it feel to fail two thousand times?' 'Young man,' said Edison, 'I didn't fail to make a light bulb two thousand times; I merely found one thousand, nine hundred and ninety-nine ways how NOT to make a light bulb.'

Imagine what life would be like if you simply looked on failure as learning how not to do something. It would completely free you up. No more beating yourself up for being no good, stupid, or a failure. Rather, you are suddenly just learning new things all the time.

When people arrive on my training courses, some have had bad experiences of learning at school, and somewhere along the line, someone has convinced them that they really aren't very bright. When I talk about there being no such thing as failure, you can visibly see them relax – it's as if all the pressure just drops away, and they are free to take some risks and experiment a bit. That doesn't mean I hand out certificates willy-nilly – they still need to do the work, and demonstrate they can work to a certain standard, but we never talk about failing. They may need to learn some ways of 'not doing it' first, and in the end, they will achieve what they set out to do.

Exercise: what would you do if you knew you couldn't fail?

Make a list of all the things you would do if you really believed that you couldn't fail. No censoring at this point. You can take baby steps here if you prefer. This is about developing your bravery muscles, so you can have whatever you want on your list.

Now ask yourself:

- ✓ 'Am I doing it?'

- ✓ 'If not, what do I need to do to get started?'

- ✓ 'How bad am I going to feel if I never try?'

Now get out there and do it! There is no substitute for this part! Starting is the hardest part, so get going and start to gather momentum! One tiny thing a day mounts up to well over 350 in a year. How would your health, your prosperity, your happiness and satisfaction with life change in a year, if you had made only one small decision or made one small action every day that would move you in the right direction?

I'm the creator of my own future

Successful happy people take their lives by the scruff of the neck. They really own it. They see the past as a resource they can learn from, and the future is within their own gift to create. Good drivers don't drive looking in the rear view mirror all the time. They glance at it to see if there is anything they need to learn, but their real focus is on where they are going. A few years back I had one of those 'big' birthdays. You know the ones when people give you experience gifts: hot air balloons, swimming with sharks at the Sea Life centre and so on? Well, I was given a gift of a driving lesson in a skid pan. When I got the safety briefing, the instructor told me that one of the most crucial things I had to remember was to look at where I wanted to go. All went well for the first few circuits, and I was congratulating myself on how easy it was. And then they squirted the slippy stuff onto the circuit, and suddenly I was rather less calm. As the back end of the car started to slide about, all I could look at was how near the wall was getting. My instructor shouted at me to look in the direction I wanted to go, but I was mesmerised with a picture of how bad it was going to be if I hit that wall. Eventually he grabbed the controls, and shouted at me to look where I wanted to go! As soon as I got control of my fear, and started to do just that, the car followed where I had placed my attention, and we were back on track.

I learned an important lesson that day – if we want to move ahead, we must stay focused on what we want. No one can do that for us.

It's more effective to start with the end in mind

Remember the 85th birthday party exercise? When we think of our purpose in life, one of the most effective ways of doing so is to think about what we want to have achieved by the end, and then ask consistently if what we are doing is getting us there. Really successful achievers take this idea one step further, and not only start with the end in mind – they actually go forwards in their heads to when they have their goal, their dream; they experience it with all their senses....... and then they look back so that they can see the entire route they took to get there. They can then use that information to help them to plan.

Installing new beliefs

What I suggest you to do now is to reflect carefully on these beliefs. Which ones do you already have in your filters? Which one will make the biggest difference to you? Are there any to which you find yourself reacting negatively? Often it's the ones that are toughest for us that will make the most difference to us when we integrate them. My invitation to you is simple: act 'as if' these beliefs are true, and as if you already have them. You can choose to let them go if they no longer serve you, but for now, pretend you believe them. As you think of yourself with these new beliefs, you might want to imagine yourself out there in your future, with some good strong beliefs in your filters, and just notice what is different.....

SETTING POWERFUL GOALS

Let's talk a bit about what you want. I don't know what the rules were in your family. Were they things like 'I want never gets' or 'Wait till you are offered' or 'Good things come to those who wait'? People are often very good at telling me what they don't want. Again and again clients will tell me they no longer want to avoid intimacy, do a job they hate, stick with an old relationship, live in the same house. If you think back to the exercise we did with the chocolate cake in the last chapter, you'll see that all this focus on what you don't want can actually cause that thing to become quite compelling to your mind. So let me ask you a simple question: 'what do you want instead?' For many of my clients, that just stops them in their tracks. They might have a few vague ideas, but rarely do people have a fully formed idea of what they do want. An exception to this was Sue.

Case study: starting with the end in mind

Sue had a serious (and I mean serious) hoarding habit. When she brought me to her house, my mouth literally fell open. The hall was piled high with newspapers, to the extent that there was only a narrow passageway to squeeze through. She hadn't been able to use her bath for years, as it was piled high with junk, and she used the tiny en-suite in her bedroom. The door of the spare room only opened enough to let a very slender person in. Carrier bags of brand new clothes were piled almost to the ceiling in her own bedroom. Unopened eBay parcels were everywhere. The kitchen had enough tinned and packet food in it to last a siege. Sue of course had other issues relating to the shopping and hoarding which we worked on, but when she did the birthday party exercise, Sue saw herself alone, as a lonely old lady, living in filth and chaos.

The only people who she ever saw were paid to be there. Children passing her house taunted her. This was an emotional exercise for Sue, and after she'd done it, she opened her eyes, and said 'Whatever it takes – I'm going to change'.

After we'd done the Wheel of Life together, Sue identified two areas she wanted to work on as a priority. One was her home, and the other was her social life. She created a very specific goal: 'In three months time, I will hold a dinner party for 6 people in my house. The house will be clean and fresh, and I will be wearing a dress and cooking for them. People will be able to move safely and freely round the house, and I'll be feeling proud of my comfortable home. I'll be laughing and chatting with them'. As an outcome went, this one had nearly everything: it had a time attached to it; it specified who would be involved and what would happen, and it had what is called an ecology check (it was to be safe). Because of this, Sue was a dream to coach. Everything she planned to do, she could ask herself the question 'Is this moving me towards my goal' and if the answer was yes, she went for it 100%. It was tough for her, and there were many tears as I coached her through the process of clearing her house, and letting go of the emotional as well as physical baggage, but she kept her goal in sight.

I visited Sue on the afternoon of the party to take her some flowers – the place was transformed. All the mess was gone, either to re-cycling, to eBay or to the charity shop. Contract cleaners had scrubbed it top to bottom, and Sue had painted the entire house in a neutral colour to give her a blank canvas for what she described as stage 2 of the transformation. Mouth watering smells came from the kitchen, the table was set with a beautiful dinner service she had found in one of the boxes, and the bathroom and lounge were inviting and warm. Later that night, Sue sent me a text. It said simply: 'Mission accomplished!'

The other important feature about goals is that they need to be for you. I can't count the number of times people come for coaching and when I ask them what they want they will say something like 'I want my husband to stop playing around' or 'I want my boss to start treating me with respect'. We cannot change what other people do, all we can change is our response to it. They may, by default, change their behaviour, but that's not guaranteed. We can't make goals for other people.

Exercise: getting to goals

So how do you go about creating compelling goals? You can do a couple of things at this point. Either go back to your possibility map, and work with something from there that you want to accomplish, or alternatively, take an area from your Wheel of Life, and have a go at working through the following questions:

- ✓ 'What do I want?' Make this positive. Do you really care about what you don't want?

- ✓ 'How will I know when I've got it?' In NLP, this is called an *evidence frame*. What will you see, hear and feel when you've achieved it? What will other people be saying about you? What will you be saying to yourself? Create a big, bright picture, with sounds and feelings. Words like 'OK' and 'nice' and that great Scottish one 'not bad' are just not going to cut it here. Be bodacious! This is your story, so make it a good one. Give your goals enough juice so you really want to get up and get at them. This is not about tinkering at the edges. You will break them down into manageable chunks later. For now, go big picture. Think of what having that goal will do for you.

- ✓ 'What else will change when I get it?' This is an important part of what is called the ecology check. Humans don't live in isolation, so check that this change improves your life overall.

- ✓ 'What resources do I already have that will help me achieve it?' These can be friends, past experiences, contacts, personal qualities – really think hard about this one, and be creative. One of the things I've learned is that many people are generous, and will give freely of time and expertise.

- ✓ 'Do I know anyone else who has done this or something similar?' Remember, if someone else has done it, then it means you already know it's possible, it's simply a matter of you learning how.

- ✓ 'What is the very first thing I need to do?'

- ✓ 'What is the very last thing that needs to happen for me to know I've achieved it?'

Excellent! You now have a well formed goal to work on. But goals without actions are just dreams. So now the real work begins!

GET MOTIVATED!

Powerful goals provide their own motivation, but sometimes you might just need that extra boost to get you going. So now you are going to add some juice to your goal, by getting yourself totally motivated to go for it. There are various ways of doing this, and I've outlined a couple below for you to try out.

Anchor your motivation

This exercise has its roots in behavioural psychology, when a stimulus and response are linked together in such a way that the moment you experience a particular stimulus, you will get the same response. We all have lots of anchors, developed over the years. Advertisers use them a lot, to attempt to link a phrase or a feeling with a product. Many of us can complete advertising jingles from our childhood, and remember the products associated with these very easily. There are lots of naturally occurring anchors: if you see a police car behind you with its light flashing for example, you will almost automatically glance at your speedometer. If you see a red traffic light while driving, you will automatically brake. I only have to smell a certain aftershave, and I am transported back to being 14, with my very first boyfriend. Sometimes we only have to see a certain look on a partner's face, and we can feel grumpy (or happy!).

In the following exercise, you are going to discover how to link motivation with a specific bodily movement, so that at any time in the future when you need motivation, you will be able to make the same movement, and access a sense of feeling motivated.

One of my students calls this exercise 'setting up the happy button'. You will already have the experience of feeling motivated to do something in the past, now you are going to put that motivation quite literally in your hand, so you can switch it on at any time.

Exercise: happy buttons

Read through the directions a couple of times, so that you are completely clear about what to do.

Think of something that you wish you felt more motivated to do, and check in with yourself that it's OK for you to feel motivated in that context.

- ✓ Give yourself a little shake, and then think of a time in the past when you were totally motivated. Make it a big, bright picture, maybe hear yourself saying 'YES!' or 'GO FOR IT!' Stand tall, and get a feeling of total, unstoppable, let-me-at-it motivation. And when you get that feeling squeeze your hand tightly into a fist.

- ✓ Repeat that cycle at least four times, each time thinking about an experience in the past when you felt totally motivated. Make a great, bright, big picture, hear yourself say 'YES!' and get a really strong feeling of motivation, while you clench your fist. Give yourself a little mental shake after each cycle.

- ✓ Now - think of the things that you need some extra motivation for, and at the same time, make a tight fist. See what you will see, hear what you will hear, and feel how wonderful you are feeling taking action.

At any time in the future, if you squeeze your fist in that way, you will get back those feelings of motivation. You can use this in different contexts, and you can feel extremely confident about the future, knowing that you have this resource quite literally in the palm of your hand!

SWISH, and there it is!

Do you ever find that you make plans for the future, but something always gets in the way, and you don't complete them? How bad does that make you feel? What would it be like to have that goal sitting right in front of your face, so it pulled you towards it the entire time? That would be pretty motivating, wouldn't it?

This is quick and easy to do, and helps you to place your goal quite literally in your sights.

Exercise: swish that goal!

If you can, it is easier to do this exercise standing up. Before you start, check in with yourself that it is appropriate for you to feel totally motivated towards your goal.

- ✓ Hold your left hand in front of you, palm facing you.

- ✓ Get a picture of what is stopping you achieving your goal, and imagine that your eyes are a digital projector. Project the image of that issue onto your left hand.

- ✓ Now get a picture of the goal. Hold your right hand up, palm facing you. Again, project that picture onto your right hand, through your eyes. Make it big, bright and appealing.

✓ Now put your left hand (with the problem) in front of you and the right hand (with the good picture) behind you.

✓ Make sure you have the old picture on your left hand, and when you are ready, rapidly (within a second), move your left hand behind your back, and bring the right one right into your visual field at the front, while making a swish sound.

✓ Repeat this up to 10 times, going faster each time, and giving yourself a little mental shake between each cycle.

✓ Put your hands down, and try to get the old picture back. What happens is that as soon as you try to think of the old picture, your goal picture will immediately flash up, so that you feel pulled towards it.

Putting your goals in your future

Sometimes the future can seem a scary, unknown place. Imagine for a moment that there is a way to get a unique perspective of your life. From that safe perspective, you can look down on your life, and see all the useful learning you can take from whatever has happened to you till this moment. And you can see your own future, and put in it exactly what you want.

Have ever had the experience of driving, or travelling, when you aren't really sure if you are going in the right direction? So many twists and turns in the road, sometimes you can't be sure that you are still going in the right direction, which way you are pointing. As you slowly drive along, looking for landmarks, perhaps you wonder if you are actually heading back the way you came. Sometimes life can be like that. So many twists, turns and obstacles to negotiate. Imagine what it would be like, though, to be able to float, high above the road. Feeling safe, comfortable and relaxed, but now with a different view. What they call a bird's eye perspective. From this position, you can see many things – where you are, where you've come from, and where you are going.

On page 84 I talked about using your memory storage system to let go of limiting beliefs. Wouldn't it be fantastic if we could create our future memories now as well? Well you can, using similar techniques.

Exercise: drawing your road-map

This exercise involves the use of time code interventions, so before you do it, you might want to go back and do the exercise on page 85 to remind you how you organise your memories.

✓ Take one of the goals you created earlier in this section. Create a picture of you having achieved that goal. Notice how you sit or stand. How do you look? What do you hear? What do you feel inside? And just notice, how far in the future is this goal? When do you want to have achieved it by?

✓ Detach from that goal, and hold it gently in your hand. Look down into your hand, and notice how you represent that goal to yourself. Some people see it as a picture, in a beautiful frame. Others see it as a precious jewel, in a velvet box. However you see it is right for you.

- ✓ And now, imagine that you are connected to that goal in some way – perhaps by a silken cord, or a velvet rope, or a golden wire – just use whatever comes. However you connect to your goal will be your guide, it can surely and irresistibly draw you towards your goal.

- ✓ Float out into your future, high above your memory storage system, until you are right at the moment where you want this goal to be achieved.

- ✓ You might want to breathe some energy onto the goal, or give it a glowing colour. Whatever works for you.

- ✓ Now slot it into place. Perhaps you even hear a click as it happens. Notice the very last thing that happened before you achieved the goal.

- ✓ Come back to the present, looking carefully at the journey between the present and your goal, so that you can notice what you have to do at various points in order to allow the goal to become a reality. So for example, if your goal is two years in the future, notice what you will need to have achieved at one year, six months, three months, next month and next week. You can slot these in as journey goals.

- ✓ When you are back in the present, look back up the line, and notice that you now have a road map which will lead you quickly and easily to your destination. Notice also that you still hold the cord, which will pull you gently forward towards your goals.

PROGRAMME YOURSELF FOR SUCCESS

People will often say to me in coaching that they find it hard to have confidence in their own abilities to make decisions. This might be especially true if they have made what they perceive as 'bad' decisions in the past, about relationships, career choices, or house moves. For some, this can become paralysing, to the extent that they never do anything, as they can't be sure that it's the right thing. Life doesn't come with guarantees though, and sometimes we do just need to take a risk.

The first thing to remember here is the 'no failure, only feedback' frame that I talked about earlier. That alone can help people feel stronger about making a decision.

> *A ship in harbour is safe, but that is not what ships are built for.*
>
> Grace Hopper

I am also a great believer in our unconscious mind (some might call this our intuition, or a gut feeling) having enormous wisdom, and if we tap into that, then it will assist us to make good decisions for us. This doesn't mean that they will always be pleasant, or easy, or even in line with what we consciously want to hear though!

This section of the book finishes with a visualisation which will help you to programme yourself for success by helping you assess the decisions you are making.

You might want to read this visualisation through a few times so that your unconscious mind can record the main points, or you might prefer to record it onto your computer.

Exercise: exploring the future

Find somewhere quiet where you won't be disturbed for 30 minutes and make yourself comfortable.

Spend a few minutes breathing in slowly through your nose, and out through your mouth until you feel relaxed and centred. When you are ready, close your eyes. If there is any unnecessary tension anywhere in your body, you can simply ..... let it go. Ask your unconscious mind to support you in coming up with a solution about your future that is just right for you.

Think for a moment about the possibility of a staircase appearing in front of you. A staircase with 10 broad, wide, shallow steps. It might be carpeted. There can be a handrail. You know that at the bottom of the steps there is something important, something you need to learn.

When you are ready, start walking slowly down the stairs, pausing for a moment on each step. With each step, you can go deeper into relaxation. Count quietly inside your head with each step you take. Starting at 10.....9.....8.....7.....more and more relaxed. More and more comfortable. Safe and relaxed. 6.....5.....into a lovely warm, relaxed place.....4......3.....feeling very good about yourself.....2.....1. Nicely relaxed and comfortable now.

Imagine that you are sitting in an art gallery, looking up at a picture. The picture has thick velvet curtains around it, in a beautiful rich colour. You feel excited, perhaps, as this is a picture you have been waiting to see for a long, long time. In your hand you hold a remote control, which you can use to open the curtains. The seat is comfortable, and you are so safe.

When you feel ready, press the button on the remote control in your hand, and open the curtains. They slide back smoothly on their runners, with a quiet swishing sound. As the curtains pull back, a spotlight comes on illuminating the picture. It is a picture of many paths, all leading out into your future. Where does each one go, I wonder? Each path leads to a different future you. How do you know which one to choose? Every moment you make choices that affect your future life.

Allow yourself to float into the picture, and hover above the paths, so your unconscious mind can see the options. It can journey along each path by itself, to its destination. It can explore carefully, and discover which paths lead you to successful, healthy, happy outcomes. Let it do that searching, while you relax now.

Your unconscious mind can do many things. Without any conscious input from you, your unconscious mind will guide you to make good decisions. Perhaps by allowing you to see, and hear, and feel, exactly what that option does for you, so that you know 'Yes. This is a good decision'.

So that you can feel more confident, more sure of yourself.

On any journey, you need resources, and provisions, and your unconscious mind can help you gather these, without any conscious involvement.

While your unconscious mind continues to travel these paths deciding what is best, you can float out of the picture now, back into your seat. Allow the picture to become foggy.

Trust that every day your unconscious mind will be searching, looking for the best possible options, guiding you carefully forward. All you need to do is to ask, and to listen.

When you feel ready, open your eyes and come back into the room, feeling brave and optimistic about your future.

CHECKPOINT

You now have in your hands some tools that will help you to create the future you want. You should now:

- ✓ Have some powerful beliefs

- ✓ Have revisited your possibility map and Wheel of Life and practised setting some great goals

- ✓ Have a happy button that gives you 'zing' and motivation every time you use it

- ✓ Be able to SWISH your way to success

- ✓ Have created a road map for your future

- ✓ Have used visualisation to explore your future.

You should still be filling in your journal with your learning as you go along, taking regular temperature readings, and checking in with your cheerleader and your Board of Advisors.

And now.....ACTION!

6

TAKE ACTION

ROUTE PLANNER

Do you have a tendency for procrastination? Are you a bit of a dreamer? Change requires action! It requires you to take consistent action, again and again, even when you don't really feel like it. In this section, you will learn powerful action planning tools. By the end, you'll have no excuses – you'll be ready to get out there and do it!

EXERCISES IN THIS SECTION

Action planning   30 minutes

ACTIONS SPEAK LOUDER THAN WORDS

This is one of the shorter sections of this book, and that's because action is something you DO. You don't think about it, or read about it, you just get off your behind and DO it.

Being good at something, and achieving what we want is first and foremost about habits. Want to write a book? Get into the habit every single day, of sitting down and writing. My commitment was 2000 words a day, but it wouldn't have mattered if it had been 200 – the point is to do something every day that will move you one step closer to what you want. Want to get fit? Then every day, take 5000 more steps than you normally do. Want to re-furbish your house? Get a new job? I'm sure you are getting the picture. Even baby steps, added together, will begin to build that new reality you want.

> *We are what we repeatedly do.*
>
> *Aristotle*

Think back to the birthday party visualisation on page 161. Everything you do today is building that future of how you will be remembered. You cannot put off living your life until you are thinner, richer, happier, until the children have grown up, until you get that new job. You have to do it now.

I was at a workshop recently and we were asked, based on our average life expectancy, to work out how many days we MIGHT have left. Even after giving myself a fairly generous expectancy of 90 years this was scary. It was for me one of the biggest wake up calls ever.

It's easy to get stuck too long in the thinking and planning phase. Yes, you may in the past have had some emotional blocks that were holding you back. Yes, in the past, you may not have had well-formed goals. In the past you might not have had all the tools you needed. But that was then. The purpose of this book was to assist you to get rid of the blocks, form the goals, and give you the tools for change and transformation. Now you have them. Now you must move into action.

So how are you going to do it? How are you (yes you!) going to take those dreams, those plans, and starting today, begin to create the future you want – totally at cause, with no more excuses?

> *Knowing is not enough, we must apply. Willing is not enough, we must do.*
>
> Johann Wolfgang von Goethe

At this point, some people will be experiencing the change transition as easy – you might be so fired up with the potential you suddenly see for transforming your life that you power forwards easily. If that is your experience, then that is fabulous, and you can probably skip the next couple of paragraphs, and go straight into taking action.

For other people, you should also start taking action, but you may find it reassuring to hear a bit about how some people experience change. For some, transition can be an uncomfortable place, where things feel out of control and you feel ill at ease. If this is your experience, then doing the relaxation exercises from Step 4 will help you get over the hump. Think of the metaphor of the butterfly. Part of the transition from caterpillar to butterfly involves struggle – if the butterfly is 'helped' out of the cocoon, it will probably be unable to fly, and it will die. Sometimes we simply need to exist in the discomfort of the transition, and trust that things will unfold as they should, and that you will emerge whole, beautiful and transformed in the same way the butterfly does.

My husband is an athletics coach. His particular area of interest is throwing events. Some time ago a parent phoned us and asked if my husband could help his son with his javelin technique before a big event he had coming up a few days later. I was really surprised to hear my husband refuse to help. He told him to carry on as normal for his competition, and then come for coaching. I couldn't believe he would miss an opportunity to help someone improve, but he explained to me that when you change someone's technique, they actually perform worse for a little while, until they integrate the changes. Not only do they need to move differently, but they need to think differently, and create new cues for different parts of the move. He said that an apparent deterioration in performance is necessary before the athlete can move on, so the boy was better to go through this phase outside of competition. As I thought about that, it made perfect sense for all sorts of changes, not just sporting ones. My experiences with many clients over the years is that it's fairly common to go through a period of dissonance when you are transforming yourself – the important thing is not to fear this, but to see it as a positive sign that things are actually shifting.

So I hope you are now totally committed to action. Let's look at some tools to help.

Action planning tools

There are two methods I find useful to spur me into action. One is a fairly organised, step-by-step activity, which suits me sometimes, the other is much more about trusting my unconscious mind to know what I need to do. I find the logical method suits me bet if I know exactly what needs to be done, have all the information, but I'm procrastinating. I prefer the second when I'm less clear about the processes involved. Try them both, and discover which you prefer.

A six-step action planning tool

This logical framework has six key steps to it:

- ✓ Decide a completion date for your goal.

- ✓ Make a commitment by telling other people who will support you.

- ✓ Identify everything that needs to happen to allow that deadline to be met.

- ✓ Decide on a set of carrots (rewards), which you will give yourself at each point in the process, after you have completed each sub task.

- ✓ Work backwards from that date, slotting all the tasks in place in order.

- ✓ Look at the first item on the list, and **do it.**

If you are prone to procrastination, you might also want to give yourself some firm pep-talks along the way to keep yourself on track.

This method worked really well for me when I was writing this book. I had done all the research, and had an outline structure, but I had been putting off starting writing. Eventually, I decided I would write it in 28 days. This meant I had to write at least 2000 words every day. I cleared my diary as far as possible, and then just went for it. I made a very public commitment by posting my plans on my Facebook page. My reward was that I posted a word count every day, and my lovely online friends all told me how fantastically well I was doing. If I ever felt I wouldn't bother on a particular day, I made a picture of how embarrassed I would feel if I had to miss my word count posting.

Asking your unconscious mind for the action plan

This method is more free-flowing than the previous one, and works well if you feel a bit stuck and don't really know how to progress. This is how you do it:

- ✓ Decide on a goal you want to focus on. All you need at this point is your goal, you don't need a plan. It can be something huge, or something every-day.

- ✓ Find a quiet place to sit where you won't be disturbed for 10 minutes. Close your eyes, and take a few slow deep breaths in through your nose and out through your mouth.

- ✓ Think carefully about what you want. Think about actually achieving the goal. Create a picture with sounds and feelings of you having achieved it. Create more and more detail in this image, until you feel a sense of energy – a sense of wanting to be getting on with it, perhaps even a sense of impatience about sitting thinking.

- ✓ Now ask yourself 'What can I do in the next 30 minutes which will move me towards this?

✓ Whatever pops into your head, you are going to do. No ifs, buts or maybes. Just accept it and take action. Open your eyes, and do it now.

If you run out of steam, just close your eyes again, take a few steadying breaths, and ask again 'what can I do now?' Again, act on the answer. A few weeks ago I created a new website using just this process. Within a day, I had all the content written and a draft design. When I thought about it before I started, though, it seemed a massive job. But broken down into 30 minute slots, it seemed manageable. There were points when the reason I couldn't move on was simply that I had a piece of information missing, and so sometimes the answer to the question 'What can I do in the next 30 minutes?' was to call a friend who is better with techie stuff than me, or to ask the question on an online forum. But everything I did moved me one step closer. The elephant that had seemed pretty indigestible at 8am had completely gone by 3pm.

> *Motivation is what gets you started. Habit is what keeps you going.*
>
> *Jim Ryun*

Exercise: action planning

Take any goal that you want to progress: if you need ideas, look back at the goal setting work you did in Step 5, or look at your Wheel of Life or your possibility map.

Choose which of the above methods suit you best for this particular goal, and use the tool to help you get to action. Ensure that you do at least the first action before you stop.

CHECKPOINT

In this section, we've looked at two action planning tools and you have started to apply them to your own goals. Carry on with this process, and record your learning in your journal.

Most importantly though, this section is about now getting out and making the changes you want to make.

The time for action is now!

7

KEEP IMPROVING

ROUTE PLANNER

This section is where we end our journey together for now. In it you will find some simple reminders to help you keep yourself moving forward. Remember that once your consciousness has been raised, it can never be lowered. Just by reading and engaging with this book, change will be happening. This section is about continuing to nurture that change.

EXERCISES IN THIS SECTION

What have I learned?   30 minutes

THE END AND A NEW BEGINNING

You and I are nearly at the end of this journey together. My intention with this book was to put tools and techniques into your hands to enable you to coach yourself. You have at your fingertips now a vast range of tools for change; tools that can help you transform yourself, and your relationships with others.

In moving forward, you might want to think about some key things, which will give you a wonderful foundation.

Build great relationships

The first and most important person to build a good relationship with is yourself. You are, after all, the one person in life you can't get away from. This means paying attention to how you talk to yourself, checking in with your inner cheerleader regularly, and trusting yourself to be able to cope with whatever appears in the attic of your unconscious mind.

Secondly, become aware of your impact on others; use assertive communication and adopt that fly-on-the-wall perspective to check out what's going on in a relationship if it gets tough.

Look after yourself

Do something every day which nourishes you mentally, physically and spiritually. This is not selfishness, it's survival. You are in fact already perfect – at worst, you've simply forgotten that. Take time to get back in touch with that inner you.

Set powerful goals

There is an ancient Zen proverb which says 'Many people spend their lives climbing the ladder, only to discover it was against the wrong wall'. It's important to spend regular time reflecting on what you really want, and self-correcting if you are drifting off-track. Ensure that your ladder is against your wall, and not someone else's. The exercises we covered about values, and your own mission and purpose in life will help you ensure this is the case. Be precise about what you want, what you will gain from having it, and how you will know when you have it. Recognise the stones that need to go into the bucket first.

Develop your senses

Get used to really noticing what you are doing and whether it is moving you in the direction you want to go. Create good pictures of what you want, talk to yourself with enthusiasm and kindness, and listen to the answers you get. Get used to checking in with any gut feelings you have. And if necessary, go back and refine your goals on the basis of that noticing.

Be flexible

The more options and choices you have in life, the greater your chances of success. Ask your Board of Advisors for suggestions, watch what you have in your filters, and practice becoming 'not you' for a while, and see where that takes you.

Take action

Goals without actions are daydreams. Be bold. No matter what your dream is, small actions every day will pull you towards it.

Audit yourself

Get into the good habit of carrying out regular audits. On a daily basis, continue to do your temperature readings and on a weekly basis, explore some key questions in your journal:

- ✓ What have I particularly enjoyed doing this week?

- ✓ What would I prefer to do more of/less of next week?

- ✓ What have I learned about myself?

- ✓ What am I going to do differently next week?

Challenge yourself

Keep pushing back the boundaries of your comfort zone, and keep adding new things to your possibility zone. Think about how you would live your life today if there were to be no tomorrow – and if you knew that you could not fail.

Celebrate your success

Perhaps already you have a different model of the world and of yourself than you did when you started this book. I hope you have developed a sense of your own personal power, and your ability to make good choices about your future, rather than allowing yourself to be tossed about on a sea of circumstances.

Some of the changes may have felt tough, some may have brought high emotion along with them. Some you may even have resisted making. Whatever you experienced, you will have learned something.

The final exercise in this book is a review.

Exercise: what have I learned?

Think about the following questions:

- ✓ What have I learned since I started this book?

- ✓ What am I most proud of?

- ✓ What has changed for me?

- ✓ What is the biggest benefit of those changes?

- ✓ What am I going to do next?

Figure 9: put your ladder on the right wall!

AND FINALLY.....

No journey is ever really complete, and the ending of one journey simply signifies the beginning of the next one. So please don't just put this book on a shelf now. My dream is that this book will become dog-eared, covered in scribbles, doodles and drips of coffee, as you use it as a manual which you refer to often. Everything in this book works – I've seen the evidence for it many times. However, it does only work if you use it. If you commit to clearing up the past; if you commit to working on your filters, and to being at cause in your life, then you will see amazing changes in your thoughts, your attitudes, your behaviour, and ultimately your results. Seek support if you need it. Be around people who are supportive of you.

> *No one can go back and make a brand new start, my friend, but anyone can start from here and make a brand new end.*
>
> *Daz Zadra*

The time is now, the power is yours. Claim it, get off your backside, and have a wonderful life!

A BIG THANK YOU AND A REQUEST

First of all, a huge thank-you to you for buying this book. I can't tell you how much that means to me. I hope you enjoyed it, and that it has given you some ideas for your own growth and development. Now I have one last request of you. If you found this book helpful, would you be willing to help promote it? You can do this in a variety of ways:

- ✓ Leave a review on www.amazon.co.uk.

- ✓ Write about it on your blog, and/or post a note about it on Facebook and Twitter.

- ✓ Recommend it to your friends.

- ✓ If you know anyone who runs a newsletter, newspaper or magazine, then I will be forever in your debt if you can write a review of the book.

- ✓ Visit me at **www.joycecampbell.co.uk** and leave a comment on my blog.

All these things would be a huge help. I'm an independent author without a huge marketing budget behind me, and as a reader you have lots of power – by helping to promote this book, then the next one can be even better.

Thank you again.

Joyce

FURTHER INFORMATION

Websites

For information about training to be an NLP practitioner, a hypnotherapist or a life coach: www.joycecampbell.co.uk. You will also find lots of additional information, CDs and tips to help you get the best from this book.

To find an NLP practitioner or an NLP coach in your area: www.inlpta.co.uk and www.anlp.org.

To find a hypnotherapist in your area: www.general-hypnotherapy-register.com and www.ukguild.com.

To find a counsellor: www.bacp.co.uk.

Books

Both my house and office are full of books, so I find it hard to select just a few. Here are some of my favourites.

Hamilton, David: *You Can Heal Your Life*. Hay House, 2008

Jeffers, Susan: *Feel the Fear and Do It Anyway*. Vermilion, 2007

O'Connor, Joseph: *Free Yourself From Fears*. Nicholas Brealey, 2005

O'Connor, Joseph and Seymour, John: *Introducing NLP*. Thorsons, 2003

Neill, Michael: *Feel Happy Now!* Hay House, 2007

Robbins, Tony: *Unlimited Power*. Simon and Schuster, 2001

Satir, Virginia: *Meditations and Inspirations*. Celestial Arts, 1985

Sharma, Robin: *Discover Your Destiny*. Element, 2004

Tracy, Brian: *Goals!* BK, 2003

Changing Mindsets & Developing Spirit

Inspirational Coaching through Verse
for Success in Sport & Life
By Helen K Emms

Available from Amazon &
www.liveitpublishing.com

There is a force in each of us that compels us to overcome our limitations and strive to experience ourselves and our life at its very best. Yet many of us struggle to be all that we can be. By changing our mind 'sets' and connecting with our Spiritual Self we can finally tap into our awesome inner power to achieve the best in whatever we desire.

Would you like to:

- Live your life with faith and without fear?
- Find contentment and deep satisfaction?
- Tap into your passion, dreams and potential?
- Develop inner strength, confidence and self-belief?
- Free yourself to connect with your Spiritual Self?
- Be who you were born to be?

If so, this beautifully written book captures the essential qualities and fundamental principles for success in sport and life. Combining her exceptional expertise in the field of peak performance coaching and personal & spiritual development, with the art of inspirational verse, **Helen K Emms** coaches us to change disempowering mindsets and nurture our spirit.

"Helen writes with intelligence, courage, passion and conviction. I was moved, challenged and empowered. Her writing is both inspired and inspiring. I urge everyone to read this gem of a book." **Patsi Hayes**, Healer, Spiritual Mentor & Author.

Also by Helen K Emms: Achieving Peak Performance in Tennis:
A Practical Guide to Developing Your Mind & Energy System for Winning.

The Essential NLP Practitioner's Handbook

How to Succeed as an NLP Therapist & Coach

By Murielle Maupoint

Available from Amazon & www.liveitpublishing.com

This is *essential* reading for all levels of NLP interest & experience and a great resource for anyone who dreams of becoming a successful Coach, Counsellor or Therapist.

The Essential NLP Practitioner's Handbook provides all the information that you need to maximise the value of your training and:

- Feel more confident in your ability to set up and run a thriving business
- Deliver professional Therapy & Coaching sessions that get great results
- Help your Clients overcome anxiety, insomnia, phobias, obesity, confidence issues and much more...

"This is an important book for NLP..."
Foreword by David Shephard, co-author of
Presenting Magically and President of the ABNLP.

"With practical guidance for setting up a successful practice, delivering effective sessions and understanding the core psychology for a range of common Client conditions, this is the only guide you need to become a highly successful Coach & Therapist." **Helen K Emms** - NLP Trainer, Psychologist, Peak Performance Coach & Author.

Lightning Source UK Ltd.
Milton Keynes UK
26 October 2010

161872UK00001B/28/P